The War Against Poetry

PRINCETON UNIVERSITY PRESS

PRINCETON, NEW JERSEY · 1970

The War Against Poetry

 *BY RUSSELL FRASER*

*This book has been
composed in Linotype Caslon Old Face
Printed in the United States of America
by Princeton University Press
Princeton, New Jersey*

FOR E.P.F., *non humilis mulier*

Words are the only defense of the mind against being possessed by thought or dream.

ELIZABETH SEWELL

No man of ripe years and of sound mind, acting freely and with his eyes open, ought to be hindered, with a view to his advantage, from making such bargain, in the way of obtaining money, as he thinks fit.

JEREMY BENTHAM

The skin and shell of things,
  Though fair,
    Are not
  Thy wish nor prayer,
    But got
  By mere despair
    Of wings.

HENRY VAUGHAN

Preface

THE SUBJECT of this book is the attack on secular verse and the theatre in England in the sixteenth and seventeenth centuries. I have sought to tell the story more comprehensively than it has been told before, and with particular attention to its social and political implications. The war against poetry, as I conceive it, is a version in miniature of the superseding of the Middle Ages by the modern world. My ultimate purpose, which I have prosecuted chiefly in terms of poetry and plays, has been to disclose the springs of this vastly consequential transition.

In reprinting passages from Renaissance books, I have normalized the spelling of *i* and *j*, *u* and *v*, and have expanded archaic contractions. In a few cases, superfluous or obsolete punctuation (for example, the stroke mark) has been omitted or altered. Italics have been dropped from quoted material, unless indicating emphasis.

The research which underlies the book was carried on chiefly in the British Museum.

I am grateful to my friends and colleagues R. S. Berman, Robert Hollander, and S. F. Johnson for reading and commenting on my writing; to my editor, Lalor Cadley, for much labor and many helpful suggestions; and to the American Philosophical Society and the National Science Foundation for their support of my work. Typing of the manuscript was subsidized by a grant from the Rackham School of the University of Michigan.

RUSSELL FRASER
Ann Arbor, 1970

Contents

The War Against Poetry

I The Husk and the Kernel

EARLY in the sixteenth century, Tyndale and Coverdale, the translators of the Bible, agree in stigmatizing poetry and popular romances as pernicious. Such truth as they convey is partial. The truth conveyed by Scripture is a plenary truth.[1] Tyndale is exercised in particular by "histories & fables of love and wantones, and of ribaudrie." A modern reader is apt to startle at the familiar examples he brings forward—books like "Robin hode and Bevis of Hampton, Hercules, Hector and Troilus." But Tyndale's concern is not so much with the intrinsic worth or lack of worth in these innocuous romances as with their fabulous character. They are "as filthy as herte can thinke" because they "corrupte the mindes of youth" with a specious version of reality.[2] That is why the Tudor humanist Roger Ascham attacks them, as also, and with greater gusto, "bookes made in Italie and translated in England." Lubricity is not in question, or not first of all, but the "carrying [of] the will to vanitie" and the seducing of "the minde with ill opinions and false judgement in doctrine."[3]

---

[1] In the phrase of a Puritan detractor of stage plays, Scripture is the "Compleat Armour against Evil Society" (title of a polemic by R. Junius, 1638).

[2] *Obedience of a Christian Man*, ? 1536, C5.

[3] *The Scholemaster*, 1570, Bk. I. For a general discussion of the English Humanist attack on romances, see R. P. Adams, "Bold Bawdry and Open Manslaughter," *HLQ*, XXIII (1959-1960), 33-48.

It is the conventional objection and it is repeated ad nauseam. What it means in part is that these hypothetically filthy books turn the reader's attention from primary to secondary business. The Elizabethan clergyman Edward Dering, who inveighs against licentious books and plays, sees a hateful analogy in this attendance on the lesser or secondary truth. He compares it to the credulous worship of "another veale" or golden calf.[4] The poets, in their endeavor to make the imposition go down, employ "fluant termes, and imbossed words, to varnish their lies and fables." The reformer Henry Crosse, who finds them out, is essaying a critique of poetical miscellanies and romances. His complaint against them is double-edged. Since they trade in circumstantial "phrases, Metaphors, Allegories, and such figurative and suparlative termes, and so much vaine eloquence," they "yeeld no fruite at all."[5]

The conjunction, as discerned by this very typical polemicist in the last year of Elizabeth's reign, is of considerable importance for subsequent times, and not least for the present. Artistic fictions are condemned on moral grounds; the critical objection is, however, to their lack of utility. The businessman or technologist— whose aims are exclusively practical—supposes, without worrying the point, that utility is paramount. The moralist employs a different vocabulary. But in his denunciation of poetry as unclean or untrue, he is invoking the same criterion. Poetry is hateful because it is occlusive or disabling. At his highest pitch, the moralist becomes the philosopher: Plato, Sir Francis Bacon, who

[4] Preface to *Brief and necessarie Catechisme or Instruction*, 1572.
[5] *Vertues Common-wealth*, 1603, Olv-2v.

4

objects to poetry as a counterfeit copy. But Bacon the philosopher is simultaneously the technologist or merely practical man. The humanist, like Sidney or like the Italian critics from whom he takes his cue, belongs in this company. The association is unexpected; it is, however, demonstrable. The humanist justifies poetry as it is an ethical discipline. Poetry is useful. In each case, utility, very amply construed, is the master motive informing the judgment of poetry and the theatre.

This is neither to embrace nor to reject altogether the modern cult of economic interpretation. "Two truths are told." Though one seems antithetic to the other, each is assimilable in the enveloping context of the new or renascent age. Economic considerations, which are translated to political activity in the seventeenth century, play a decisive role in the attack on the stage. But the attack is prompted also by a powerful and revolted sense of concupiscent man, and a desire to fire out the worser angel to which this fallible creature is yoked. The animus of the Puritan, as of the entrepreneur, manifests, however, only a corner of the new psychology which distinguishes the present from the past. This psychology is utilitarian, but not uniquely in the narrow sense of self-aggrandizement. What is crucial—to the financier like Sir Thomas Gresham; or to the jurist like Edward Coke; or the Calvinist theologian like William Perkins or William Ames; or the propagandist of new science like Bacon or John Webster or Bishop Sprat—is the impulse to refine or to rationalize: to come to the kernel. The more profitable activity which the reformers are commending, as against

5

the fruitless cultivating of poems and plays, is identified with an apprehending of the plenary truth.

The identification is not new in the sixteenth and seventeenth centuries. Early in the twelfth century, a Scholastic philosopher wishes to know how the soul is profited by "the strife of Hector, the arguments of Plato, the poems of Virgil or the elegies of Ovid."[6] The same question occurs to Plato himself, in attacking poetry as the father of lies. Only it is urged more insistently now, and often with an eye to material satisfaction, as the possibility of coming to the heart of the matter is estimated with greater optimism than men had dared evince before.

To the new optimist, what is untrue is disgusting, especially as it is unfruitful. The poem or romance is a figure, and therefore mendacious. The conclusion, more strident than hitherto as the age is more hopeful and purposive, is to avert the eyes from the spastic playing of puppets, "where there is much stir to little purpose, till the Play be ended,"[7] and proceed to the building of the kingdom.

The customary treatment of the attack on poetry and plays, as it fails to account for the ultimate ground of the attack, is, on my view, a simplistic treatment. Those whom Sir Philip Sidney calls the *Mysomousoi* or poet-haters are supposed to be animated exclusively by moral fervor; an allegiance to Puritanism or to its earlier manifestations describes them. This point of view is

[6] Honorius of Autun, preface to *Gemma Animae, c.*1120, in J.W.H. Atkins, *English Literary Criticism*, p. 69.

[7] Richard Baxter, quoted in William Haller, *The Rise of Puritanism*, p. 101.

enunciated in the pioneering study of the campaign to close the theatres.[8] It has been challenged only infrequently since.[9] But the hatred of poetry is not peculiar to the Puritan. The bigotry of those who give expression to this hatred is without question sincere. It is engendered, however, not so much by a horror of license, whether real or imagined, as by a horror of imposition. The golden calf of the preacher anticipates the stuffed ox of Prometheus, which Bacon presents as "aping the form but wanting the substance," and hence as interven ing between men and their appointed business.[10] This business is the detecting and the harnessing of truth.

Sometimes moral fervor serves an end beyond itself. Here, to make the point, is a complementary illustration. Toward the middle of the eighth century, Pepin the Short, the son of Charles Martel, succeeds his father as mayor of the palace and ruler of the Frankish dominions. About the same time, Anglo-Saxon missionaries under St. Boniface begin their attempt to Christianize the pagan Germans beyond the Rhine. The Papacy, in its efforts to convert the Lombards, had

[8] E.N.S. Thompson, *The Controversy between the Puritans and the Stage*. The conventional point of view is expressed succinctly by Tucker Brooke in *A Literary History of England*, p. 443: "The whole business looks like a peculiarly trivial 'war of the theatres,' except as it reveals the deep abiding sense of moral fragility out of which Puritanism grew." The position developed by W. Holden in *Anti-Puritan Satire* is essentially the same: "The core of the argument to 1642 is beyond question religious . . . political and economic considerations, although they are present, are subservient to the real issue, the correct manner for worshipping God" (p. ix).

[9] For example, by William Ringler in his biography of Stephen Gosson.

[10] *The Advancement of Learning*, 1605, Bk. iii, Ch. iii.

7

received no assistance from Charles Martel. Pepin, who is ambitious of annexing the Frisians and Thuringians and Bavarians and Saxons, renders important assistance to St. Boniface. That is not to impugn his piety.

The suggestion of ulteriority is implicit, sometimes it is clamant, in the strictures of the Renaissance reformer from the Henrician period to the advent of the Commonwealth. This tiresome person is worth quoting at some length, that one may emphasize in what he says a consistent bias that has gone largely unremarked by the literary historian. It is, for example, in his character of iconoclast that the Puritan divine Richard Rogers repudiates "vaine, idle, unsavory and unprofitable bookes and Pamphlets."[11] He "scornes to preferre the Case before the Instrument, the Rinde before the Pith." A moralizing poet of the seventeenth century gives him his rubric: "substance before appearance."[12] In the opinion of a successful entrepreneur like Sir John Melton, who is writing early in the reign of James I, "they which once fal into the humour of vercifing . . . [are] to men duely conversant in weightie and profitable affaires . . . flat and tedious." Melton, whose profit accrues mostly from the vending of coal and saltpeter, thinks that poets "may bee placed among the number of shitle-cocks, tennis-balles, apes, munkies, baboones, parrats [and] puppets." The association is inevitable in the context of a purposive age. Pecunia, says Ben Jonson in the *Staple of News*, is "the Venus of our time and state." The poet, as he offers at a dif-

[11] *The Practice of Christianitie*, 1618, p. 345.
[12] Richard Brathwait, *The English Gentlewoman*, 1631, pp. 7, 115.

ferent shrine, has "correspondence to no . . . [fruitful] use & purpose."[13]

The Jacobean businessman, who measures utility in terms of avoirdupois, is sufficiently coarse; Max Weber might have invented him. The preacher, whose criteria are ethical and moral, is not so obvious in formulating his indictment. The scientist and social critic—Galileo, Jean Bodin, to whom poetry is ephemeral and therefore indifferent—are more elusive than the preacher. But the gravamen of these various objections is the same. Poetry, which takes a mess of shadows for its meat, is rejected as it is useless.

The drama allows a physical dimension to the representation of chimeras, and is in this respect more pernicious than popular fiction. An Oxford theologian in the second half of the sixteenth century attacks what he calls "the sights and shewes of theaters" precisely as they are chimerical. "Whatsoever things are true," he admonishes his readers, "think ye on these things."[14] Since corporeality is the province of the theatre, "all Plaies, as carnall, be obscene and ridiculous."[15] The playgoer, as he makes much of these carnal fictions, is a "wit-blinde gull" who "in lieu of delicies" or more

[13] A Sixe-Folde Politician, 1609, pp. 32f., 36. Poetry "may be termed the mushroom conceptions of idle braines." It is "begotte over night in tobacco smoake and muld-sacke, and uttered and delivered to the worlds presse by the helpe & midwifery of a caudle the next morning." With the quotation from Jonson, cf. Henry Peacham (The Worth of a Penny, 1647): "now money is the world's god. . . . Pecunia omnia obediunt" (cited in L. C. Knights, Drama & Society in the Age of Jonson, p. 123).

[14] John Rainolds, preface to Six Conclusions Touching the Holie Scripture, 1584.

[15] Osmund Lake, A Probe Theologicall, 1612, p. 269.

9

substantial delights "will swallow guilded Flies." Like the Egyptians in their fog, he is "hoodewinkt"—it is the apposite word—"with the condensate and cloudy night of ignorance."[16]

To the age which has been granted a vision of the plenary truth, this hoodwinking, in which the artist participates, is especially odious. The clergyman Francis Meres, who is not averse to poems and plays, affirms the characteristic impatience of Renaissance man with superficies. In compiling his list of diverting romances "to be censured of" (*Palladis Tamia*, 1598), Meres is concerned, not to censure impartially, but to separate the wheat from the chaff or the fruit from its profitless cover. The same concern is decisive for the Cambridge Puritan Dudley Fenner, who is seeking to distinguish between *Lawfull and Unlawfull Recreations* (1587). The surface of things is secondary to the "clusters of grapes" that lie beneath (Meres).[17] Or else the surface, though it presents "a shewe of godliness," lulls us "into such a sleepe, as doeth . . . make . . . [us] slouthfull and idle to all goode workes" (Fenner). For this reason, "we are expresly forbidden to take up the outward fashion" or commit ourselves to "fayning the outwarde shewes whiche are used in playes."

The kind of imitation the preceptor is rebuking in the theatre is only "of the jesture, behaviour, or speech of evill men." So far his hostility to art is contingent. But already this hostility has begun to ramify, as in the maledictions of Barnabe Googe, a drab poet of the pe-

[16] J. H., *This Worlds Folly*, 1615, B2v.
[17] Quoted in G. G. Smith, *Elizabethan Critical Essays*, II, 308f.

riod just before Spenser. Googe, who is translating an
early sixteenth-century opponent of the empirical phi-
losophy of Aristotle, is more sweeping in his prohibition,
and possibly more logical. It seems to him futile to
winnow the wheat from the chaff. As he contemplates
"verses filthy to be namde, which . . . [men] should
eschew" and do not, he makes up his mind to "defye
both verse, and Poetes al as one."[18]

To reprehend all poems and poets is, from the point
of view of the root-and-branch reformer, the only tena-
ble position. "Destruction," in the judgment of the
reforming clergyman Osmund Lake, "groweth . . . from
the eares taking in the forme of corrupting words."[19]
The modifier is, however, superfluous, as the homiletic
writer Richard Brathwait perceives. It is simply in the
nature of "words [to] corrupt the disposition; they set
an edge or glosse on depraved Liberty: making that
member offend most, when it should be imployed in
profiting most. The tongue," says this pious but hard-
headed man, "is more effectual than any Letter."[20]

What is at issue, for example to the Reverend Ed-
ward Dering, is the abhorrence of words as words: and
this, even though the typical polemicist is not inclined
to be niggardly in the use of words. "Bookes of so great
vanitie," like *Tottel's Miscellany* or like the *Court of
Venus*, are to be burned, not merely as they are "un-
chaste" but as the poets who sponsor them speak "like
the Parrets, in wordes without understanding." Dering

[18] *The Zodyake of lyfe* [Palengenius], trans. 1560, A7-v.
[19] *Probe Theologicall*, p. 267.
[20] *English Gentlewoman*, p. 139.

thinks that "Wee have nowe long inough played with our owne fancies."[21] Like Bacon, he is counseling an advance to the palace of the mind. It is not, or not simply, *saeva indignatio* but the desire to pass by the glozing copy—the stuffed ox of Prometheus—that inclines the Puritan controversialist to interdict "Love-Songs, amarous Bookes, filthy Ballads, Enterludes . . . [and] Lascivious representations of Love-Matters in Playes and Comedies."[22] The authority he alleges and the way he construes it underline his contempt for superficies. With respect to "filthy speeches," to which all artistic endeavor is explicitly referred, "the Rule of the Apostle is generall, *Abstaine from Every evill shewe*."

At first the drama is spared from this general anathematizing. That is attributable to its religious origin, as also to the didactic or heuristic approach it develops. It is not until the 1570s in England that stage plays begin to be classified among unregenerate forms of entertainment, as in Stephen Gosson's "short Apologie . . . against Poets, Pipers, Players, & their Excusers" (1579).[23] The first wholesale condemnation of the drama occurs (so far as I can tell) on November 3, 1577, in a Sunday sermon delivered at Paul's Cross in London. (This was the destination toward which Essex was making on a Sunday morning in February a little more than two decades later, in the wan hope of

[21] Preface to *Brief Catechisme*.

[22] *The Summe of Sacred Divinitie,* ? 1630, O6 (attributed erroneously to John Downhame; author unknown).

[23] Hardin Craig, following Ringler, dates the attack on the theatres as beginning, precisely, in 1577: *English Religious Drama*, p. 354. Chambers, *Elizabethan Stage*, I, 244, locates the first signs of hostility in 1561 and 1564.

12

arousing the congregation against the Queen at White-
hall. Essex, unlike the preacher, fails as he is insuffi-
ciently quixotic.) Convention dictates the matter of the
sermon. The audience will expect to be edified by a
discourse on the wickedness of bearbaiting or the flout-
ing of the sumptuary laws or the moral significance of
portents and prodigies, like the freezing over of the
Thames or the waxing in brilliance of a vagrant star,
like the nova of 1572. On this particular Sunday, the
preached abandons the staple sort of homiletic chest-
nuts. London in 1577 is gripped by plague. The cause
of plague is sin. And now the new departure: "the
cause of sinne are playes: therefore the cause of plages
are playes."[24]

This heartfelt non sequitur is important for the fu-
ture. In the following year the attack on plays is re-
sumed in sermons by John Stockwood and John Wal-
sal. Before the month is out, the Reverend John North-
brooke begins a formal treatise in reproof of the stage
and "other idle pastimes" and so initiates a polemical
contest of major proportions and decisive and cata-
strophic results. This contest, which is fought out for
more than half a century, culminates at last in the over-
whelming victory of the party of reform. On Septem-
ber 2, 1642, Parliament ordains the closing of all thea-
tres in England. "Whereas," runs the edict which puts
a period to the Renaissance drama, "the distracted estate
of England, threatened with a cloud of blood by a civil
war, calls for all possible means to appease and avert
the wrath of God . . . it is therefore thought fit and
ordained by the Lords and Commons in this Parliament

[24] T. W., *A Sermon Preached at Pawles Crosse*, pub. 1578, C8-v.

assembled, that, while these sad causes and set times of humiliation do continue, public stage-plays shall cease and be forborne." It is true that the theatres are permitted to reopen with the return of the monarchy a generation later. But in the heat and introspection of long-protracted controversy a new attitude is forged: toward the stage and, by extension, toward literature in general, and the language and spirit in which plays and poems are written and the business with which they are properly concerned. This attitude is manifest not only in the Puritan but also in the poet and playwright.

Caroline London is able to support a half dozen theatres; Restoration London scarcely two. Theatres like the Globe and Swan accommodate a vast audience of 3,000 people. This audience is drawn from all classes of society: from the *lumpenproletariat* whom Giordano Bruno describes in a vivid and terrible reminiscence of London, but also from the merchant class and the lawyers and apprentices and students of the Inns of Court. Mistress Quickly is a patron of the harlotry players; so is Duke Philip Julius of Stettin-Pomerania. When, early in the reign of James I, Shakespeare's company takes over the private playhouse of Blackfriars (1608), that is felt to be an eccentric transaction: excepting the King's Men, all the adult companies in London are associated with the public theatres. Early in the reign of Charles I, the association is dissolved. The better sort give their allegiance to the Phoenix or Blackfriars or, later, to the Salisbury Court; the Globe and Fortune and Red Bull are reserved to the rank-scented many. The public audience—"Squirrels that want Nuts," as the dramatist James Shirley describes it—is already a contradiction in terms. "Sit," he says condescendingly—he is addressing the descendants of those various patrons for whom Shakespeare wrote his plays—

> As you were now in the *Black-Friers* pit;
> And . . . [do] not deaf us, with leud noise and tongues,
> Because we have no Heart to break our Lungs.[25]

Shirley knows that the Bankside is "far more skilfull at the Ebbes and flows / Of water, than of wit." On the hypothetically more sophisticated understanding of this Caroline writer, the theatre is a private pastime. Essentially, that is what it has remained ever since.[26]

Restoration comedy is the last great efflorescence of the English drama, before the advent of Shaw and Oscar Wilde and John Millington Synge fully two hundred years later. Its appeal is, however, restricted, and by design. The poet and playwright Sir Charles Sedley detects in his colleague Thomas Shadwell very little concern to amuse or instruct the middle classes: "You," as he salutes them, "who had never yet, / Either your Heads or Bellies full of wit."[27] But these middle class persons are not listening anymore.

Partly, the animosity of the Puritans and their allies is inspired by the relatively new and burgeoning popularity of the theatre. Popular patronage increases dramatically with the construction, by James Burbage in 1576, of the first public building in England dedicated explicitly to the performing of stage plays. The opening of the Theatre and, a few months later, the Curtain gives enormous impetus to the popularity of plays. An-

---

[25] Prologue to *The Doubtful Heir*, 1640.

[26] Discussion draws on G. E. Bentley, *Shakespeare and His Theatre*, pp. 127, 103.

[27] Prologue to *Epsom Wells*, 1672.

ciently, the drama is committed to a fugitive existence, mounted in the great hall of a nobleman's manor or in an innyard or college refectory or, more rarely, at Court, or in the private precincts of the law schools. The players are strolling players who, as a Puritan pamphleteer is eager to report, are "taken by the Lawes of the Realme, for roagues and vacabounds."[28] In a popular verse satire written in the early years of the century, players are consigned to the disreputable fellowship of tumblers and jugglers and pickpockets and debasers of the coinage.[29] Burbage at a stroke makes them over. From itinerants outside the pale, on whom the censorious are able to visit a negligent contempt, they are metamorphosed to permanent members of a repertory company, playing at fixed intervals and in a settled and commodious place. "How chances it they travel?" Hamlet inquires. "Their residence, both in reputation and profit, was better both ways."

This bettering does not pass without notice. From the 1570s forward, the reformer reserves his fiercest hatred for the drama: not as he hates poetry less but as he fears the drama more. In fact this hatred is impartial. It is extended progressively to cover and to interdict all forms of art as the impulse grows irresistible to apprehend the kernel of things. The campaign to close the theatres and the war against poetry are one. Each, as it affects to show "the very age and body of the time his form and pressure," is beguiled by the particular exemplification. This general banning of literature as imposition is endorsed by the anonymous crackbrain who,

[28] Philip Stubbes, *The Anatomie of Abuses*, 1583, N6.
[29] *Cocke Lorell's Bote*, 1510.

16

in the year of Shakespeare's death, fashions a *Covenant between God and Man* in which "stage-playing and enterludes" are represented as "Satans shop or schoolehouse to bring up prentices and young Scholers to the Art and mystery of whoredome and Adultery." What goes on in this schoolhouse is instructive: it is "foule and wicked words . . . gestures and actions . . . filthy communication."[30] But these "terms and words of art," as they are intrinsically specious, have no issue in light or labor.

Here, the impersonal zeal for the primary truth is reinforced powerfully by pragmatic considerations. "There are tenne sinnes," on the count of the London preacher Robert Hill, "which like so many Monopolizing ingrossers, doe take up all the houres of mans life: The first is Reading of vaine Bookes."[31] This cardinal sin is more heinous as the hours it dissipates are felt as golden hours, and not least in material terms. Believing that "the principall scope of all our actions and counsels, ought to be to some good ende," the moralist Henry Crosse sees how "it must consequently follow, that all prophane and lascivious Poems, are as an infectious aire, that brings a generall plague."[32] The stark delineating of "honest plain matter" without resort to "Poeticall additions or faigned Allegories" is commendable on esthetic or philosophical grounds. I have "bluntly spoken what I have observed," says the plain stylist George Wither.[33] In this, he consults his own pleasure.

[30] By I. F., 1616, pp. 381-83 (Bb 7-8).
[31] *The Pathway to Prayer, and Pietie*, 1613, R1.
[32] *Vertues Common-wealth*, O3v.
[33] Preface to *Abuses Stript, and Whipt*, 1613.

But profit is anterior to pleasure. The stripping away of excrescence is also conceived as availing or enabling, and in the present time. For this reason, the obscurity associated with art becomes, in the Renaissance, a burning issue. "All things are lawfull unto me, but all things profite not": that is Dudley Fenner, after St. Paul.[34] The observation is admonitory. It means, in this context, that profit will determine admissibility or use. "A feast is made for laughter, and wine maketh merry: but money answereth all things." To Fenner, concluding his treatise on *Recreations*, the sentence of the Wiseman (10:19) comes naturally to mind. Now, "Nothing is lawful but that which tendeth to the glory of God, and the profit of man in comelinesse."[35] *Quid dant artes nisi luctum et laborem?* To the devotee of what is palpably useful, that is the indicated question. In the early years of the seventeenth century, it is reiterated with dreadful persistence.

In support of his opinion "that there is not a greater Mart in the universall world for the Divels wares, then is the Stage," the author adduces the pagan provenance of stage plays, the (necessary) resort in the theatre to transvestism, and, critically, the pronouncements of the early Church in Council, as also of the earlier Fathers: for example, St. Cyprian, Tertullian, and St. John Chrysostom. That is the standard to which he rallies his supporters, and in this it typifies the considerable library of eristic literature directed against the stage in the later sixteenth and seventeenth centuries. The ob-

[34] *Recreations*, A4.
[35] Henry Crosse, P2.

18

jections are formulaic. They function essentially as a blind.

These polemical writings recapitulate what is or what looks to be the familiar story of an unintelligent and bigoted affiliation to the letter that kills. William Crashaw, the father of the poet, warns us to "take heede of the Theatre, where (if the olde Fathers may be trusted) a man can hardly escape acquaintance with the Divell." Given the authority of the Fathers, Crashaw is willing to accept on faith "our daily and dreadful experience."[36] He is the type of the dutiful acolyte. "So Tertullian. So wee also." That is the conventional sequence, as developed by the Caroline preacher Henry Burton in a notorious critique of the stage.[37] The very popular tractate by Philip Stubbes (*Anatomie of Abuses*, 1583) is pretty much a boiling down of classical and patristic objurgations. William Prynne, in all his vast condemnation of stage plays (*Histriomastix*, 1632), touches only infrequently on the contemporary theatre. The loss of his ears does not signify to Prynne: what he knows is gathered mostly from books, in his case from the pronouncements of the Fathers. Nor is the clergyman Osmund Lake, in directing against the stage a *Probe Theologicall upon the Commandments*, writing from scandalized experience. It is erudite hearsay that informs his attack. Each argument he puts forward is buttressed or established by marginal reference to Holy Writ or to the patristic or classical writers or to the men of Reform, like Beza and Peter Martyr. If he discovers illegality "in Enterludes, in stage-plays, in May-

---

[36] *The Parable of Poison*, 1618, p. 9.
[37] *For God, and the King*, 1636, p. 91.

gaddings; and especially in Dancings, where Tib and Tom keepe hoite together under a Summer-lug," that is because he is remembering St. Paul.[38] Ostensibly, the "profitable questions" he agitates are rooted in contemporary abuses. He has learned of "a pitifull case, at Paul's Cross reported, of a formerly very sober and chaste Matrone in London, whom ill egging drew to the Theater," and with the result that "she became afterward a notorious strumpet."[39] But anecdotage, however lurid, is not so much to the purpose as a knowledge of "the doctrine of the law." This antique knowledge is not properly Jacobean. Neither is the psychology nor the animus of the writer. Really what he is reflecting is the psychology of the ante-Nicene Church. That is on the face of it a mysterious fact.[40]

The hostility of the primitive Church is both virulent and rationalizable. The Desert Father Paphnutius implies it in his humble saying that "no one in this world ought to be despised, let him be a thief, or an actor on the stage."[41] In this ultimate compassionating, the actor sees where he stands. Early in the fourth century, the Church, speaking in Council, forbids women to marry actors or to lend them their garments. On the edict of

[38] Romans 13:13; *Probe*, pp. 95, 116.

[39] *Probe*, p. 267.

[40] Chambers, *Elizabethan Stage*, I, 255, states that attacks on the theatre were prompted by contemporary abuses: "The main burden of the complaints raised by the Puritans rested neither on theology nor on history, but on the character of the London plays as they knew them, and on the actual conditions under which representations were given." The polemical literature of the period overturns this position.

[41] Rufinus tells the story in *Historia Monachorum*; Helen Waddell, *The Desert Fathers*, p. 51.

a subsequent Council, excommunication is denounced against Christians who go on the stage. Clergymen are to have no traffic with it. The homilies of St. John Chrys ostom, written in the same century, castigate impartially the actor and the auditor who, as he patronizes the stage, "taking delight, and laughing, and praising what is done, and in every way gaining strength for such workshops of the devil," is even more to be censured than the harlot women and buffoons "who act these scenes of adultery."[42]

This virulence is plausible; I suppose it is inevitable: until the sixth century, actors are universally pagan; the plays they enact are idolatrous and anti-Christian in spirit. The Roman theatre satirizes Christianity and is very reasonably condemned by Christian polemicists from the time of Tertullian forward (*De Spectaculis*). The condemnation of the stage, as voiced by St. Augustine in the opening book of the *City of God*, is explicable mostly in terms of moral fervor. The statement holds very generally of Augustine's contemporaries and successors, almost to modern times. What is disconcerting to Bishop Isidore of Seville, early in the seventh century, is not the showing of a mirror to nature; it is the barbaric spectacles of the Roman stage.

The reformers of the English Renaissance cannot plead in their attacks even this reminiscent justification. The point is worth laboring a little. The animus against the stage, as expressed by the early Fathers, is logical in that it is addressed to a real and particular grievance. The sharp recurring of this animus in the Renaissance

---

[42] Homily VI on the Gospel of St. Matthew; Vol. x, pp. 42f. in *Ante-Nicene, Nicene, and Post-Nicene Fathers.*

is not logical at all, or not on its face. The pagan theatre no longer exists: the modern reformer has (apparently) no legitimate target. As that is so, his extraordinary ferocity seems almost as puzzling as repellent. I will take "thy suckyng babes and dashe them to the stones": that is John Hall, the moralizer of secular verse, on the fate he intends for his opponents.[43] When Stephen Gosson in *Playes Confuted* (1590?) retorts on the wan apologies of Thomas Lodge and the actors, it is not the pertinent present to which he goes for his exempla but the remote and inapplicable past. Tertullian in the second century deprecates the stage; Gosson levies on Tertullian. *Da magistrum*, he says—like St. Cyprian who, as he venerates Tertullian, pleads the same reasons in restating his master's prohibition of plays.[44] In his slavish pleading, he affords the Elizabethan polemicist, who has no reasons which sense will honor, a motto for his title page. This motto is felicitous: *Non diserta, sed fortia.* Gosson is not eloquent; he is, however, strong. But his is the strength of opacity, which blinds as it emboldens.

Evidently he requires much boldness. Existence as he sees it is a marching to war, darkling in its issue and fought for an everlasting guerdon. "Behinde, before, we no where lacke a foe"[45]: in this tremulous saying Gosson's fearful but resolute position is conveyed. Like Luther, he hypothesizes sinister spirits conspiring for his doom or demons roaming the earth or riding the

[43] *The Court of Virtue*, 1565, F8.

[44] F. W. Farrar, *History of Interpretation*, p. 180. Cyprian's restatement is given in the Epistle to Donatus.

[45] *Court of Virtue*, C6.

22

winds, waiting to snatch the unwary.[46] Eleven men in buckram materialize out of nothing. It may be so dark that he cannot see his hand; still he knows himself "mightily beset with heapes of adversaries."[47] It is not surprising if the good man, who looks incessantly to his armor, is apt to seem hysterical. "Everything," says Luther, "is full of devils, in the courts of princes, in houses, in fields, in streets, in water, in wood, in fire."[48] Gosson is only more prolix. "Certaine it is," he affirms, "that this life of ours is a continuall warrefare, a pitchte fielde, wherein, as the lickerous tongue of our mother Eve hath justly provoked the Lorde, to set the devill and us at deadly feude, so is it our part to bethinke us of him, that never leaves nibling at our heele."[49]

So dramatic or melodramatic a vision of life allows of no quarter to the adversary, for if he prevails against us we are surely damned. The death of Christopher Marlowe is good tidings to his contemporary Edmund Rudierde. Marlowe is "a Poet, and a filthy Play-maker," one of those who puts rancors in the vessel of our peace. "This wretch," says Rudierde, "accounted . . . Moses to be but a conjurer, and our sweete Saviour but a seducer, and a deceiver of the people." It is the playwright who is deceived.

> But harken yee braine-sicke and prophane Poets, and Play-ers, that bewitch idle eares with foolish vanities: what fell upon this prophane wretch, having a quarrell against one

[46] Quoted in R. H. Bainton, *The Reformation of the Sixteenth Century*, p. 26.

[47] Dedication to *Playes Confuted*, ? 1590.

[48] *Sämmtliche Schriften*, xiii, 1259; xxii, 1917; quoted in N. O. Brown, *Life Against Death*, p. 212.

[49] *Playes Confuted*, B5.

23

whom he met in a streete in London, and would have stabbed him. But the party perceiving his villainy prevented him with catching his hand, and turning his owne dagger into his braines, and so blaspheming and cursing, he yeelded up his stinking breath: marke this yee Players, that live by making fooles laugh at sinne and wickednesse.[50]

This same passionate and myopic intensity characterizes the pamphleteer Philip Stubbes, who is moved by the collapse of Paris Garden (January 13, 1583) to meditate exultantly on the victims with their "heads all to squasht." Of the thousand persons who attend the bearbaiting, every third "at the least," according to John Field, another Puritan divine, is "maimed and hurt." Field is assuaging his disappointment at what appears to be a tempering of the wind.[51] In the next century, a more dreadful event overtakes the audience at a performance of the old, and blameless and tedious, comedy of *Mucedorus* (February 3, 1652). Anatomizing this catastrophe, the Reverend John Rowe discovers in it the *Wonderfull hand of God* (1653). With "the Crack of the beame . . . and the fall of the Chamber" in which the comedy is played—I quote from Rowe's relation—there bursts forth "a fearfull, and most lamentable cry, some crying . . . aid for the Lord's sake, others crying Lord have mercy on us, Christ have mercy on us," and others "oh my Husband! . . . or my Wife! a third Oh my child! and another said No body loves me so well as to see where my child is." But what distresses the moralist is not the sight of parents carrying

---

[50] *The Thunderbolt of Gods Wrath*, 1618, E3.

[51] *Godly Exhortation by occasion of the late judgement of God*, 1583.

"home their Children dead in their armes" but the escape of the wretched transvestite. According to Rowe, "the man in womans apparell lay panting for breath" and had certainly "been stifled; but Bremo [his fellow actor] having recovered himself a little, bare up the others head with his arme, whereby he got some breath, and so was preserved." In the face of this inopportune resuscitation, it is necessary to suppose that God "hath reserved the great and full recompense for another day and place."[52]

The detractor of stage plays, as he wishes to return to the beginnings of the faith, participates enthusiastically but apparently without logic in the more substantive prejudice that marks those beginnings. What begets this unlikely participation? The greatest dramatist of the age embodies in his plays a view of the world and man's business in it that seems to me profoundly Christian. That does not matter. Within a year of Shakespeare's death, an English Catholic ecclesiastic, faithful in spirit to the new exclusivism that comes in with the Reformation, forbids all secular priests within his jurisdiction to go to the theatre anymore.[53] Already in Shakespeare's youth, the Puritan preacher Thomas Sparke, in a Rehearsal Sermon at Paul's Cross (1579), denounces the theatre as a "sinke of al sinne." Two years later, an anonymous tractarian asserts, in a Treatise of Daunses, "that they are as it were accessories and dependants . . . to whoredom," and that "playes are joyned and knit

---

[52] T. S. Graves, "Notes on Puritanism," SP, XVIII (1921), 154-57.

[53] Folger MS 4787: "Prohibition of William Harrison, archpriest, forbidding secular priests to attend the theatres, March 9, 1617."

together in a ranck or rowe with them." Bishop Gervase Babington, in what purports to be a *Very Fruitful Exposition of the Commandements* (1583), deplores the theatre as a sexual excitant. The finger of scorn is pointed at "prophane & wanton stage playes or interludes," as they are the supposed occasion "of adultery and uncleanenesse by gesture, by speech, by conveyances, and devises to attaine to so ungodly desires."[54] The schoolmaster and writer on orthography, Francis Clement, delineating his picture of "adulterous playes," perceives that the root of evil is watered on the Southbank.[55] It is the discovery of the metre balladmongers who detect in the London earthquake of April 6, 1580 evidence of God's displeasure with the theatre, and are moved to write broadsides like *Comme from the plaie*. (As it happens, this celebrated disaster claims the lives of only two victims, who are attending a sermon in Christ Church.)[56]

John Selden, perhaps the greatest scholar of the age, honors an anxious request from his friend Ben Jonson that he examine the Biblical objection to exchange of apparel. According to Deuteronomy (22:5), a text the reformers never tire of urging against the stage, "the woman shall not wear that which pertaineth unto a man, neither shall a man put on a woman's garment." That is abomination in the sight of the Lord. Selden concludes, however, that this terrible prohibition is founded entirely on its connection with pagan worship. The connection no longer obtains. That does not matter either. Henry Crosse in his pedantry has located a musty text,

54 P. 316.　　　　　55 *The Petie Schole*, 1587.
56 Chambers, *Elizabethan Stage*, IV, 208.

26

and it suffices: "It is no small offence (saieth Ciprian) for a man to disguise himselfe in the garments of a woman."[57] William Ames adduces Scripture, in declaring that for men to "put on Womens apparell, face, and gesture . . . is repugnant to the word of God."[58] When the Oxford cleric John Rainolds attacks an academic play by his colleague William Gager (1591), he is mostly concerned—or at least on the surface—that the playwright should be a party to the dressing up of men in women's clothing.[59] It is no wonder Shakespeare is moved to lament that fortune "did not better for my life provide / Than public means which public manners breeds."

Good manners are wanting in the attack on the stage. Evidently rational argument is wanting also. The Fathers have reason, in drawing up their indictment; the reformers who emulate them seem impelled only by mindless antiquarian zeal. Chrysostom in the fourth century is close enough to pagan times to feel the point of the Biblical injunction.[60] Where is the point a thousand years later? Is there, in the strictures of Stephen Gosson and the Calvinist theologian William Perkins, nothing but a dreary and foolish consistency?[61] I think

[57] *Vertues Common-wealth*, Q3.

[58] *Conscience, with the Power and Cases Thereof*, 1639, p. 216.

[59] *Th' Overthrow of Stage-Playes*, 1599. The Rainolds-Gager controversy is recapitulated in Chambers, *Elizabethan Stage*, I, 251-53; and in Karl Young, *Transactions*, XVIII, pp. 593-638. Young, pp. 604-37, reprints Gager's defense. F. S. Boas, *University Drama*, pp. 244-48, describes the similar controversy between Rainolds and Albericus Gentilis.

[60] Homily XXXVII on the Gospel of St. Matthew; x, 249 in *Ante-Nicene, Nicene, and Post-Nicene Fathers*.

[61] Third Action of *Playes Confuted*; *Cases of Conscience*, 1595.

there is more substantial content in these strictures than a cursory inspection discloses.

The dead letter of an earlier day is canonized in the teeth of the fact. Theodosius the Great, in the waning years of the Roman Empire, bans plays on the Sabbath as part of his program to ferret out pagan survivals and institute an orthodox Christian state. In the late sixteenth century, preachers and polemicists like John Field and William Rankins, John Norden and Philip Stubbes, and—a peculiar conjunction—the poet George Whetstone, all of them precisians in conning the letter, concur in the prohibition of 385 A.D.[62]

The contemporary stage is a replication of the pagan *spectacula*: that is the ground of the concurrence. Its pedantry (inapplicability) is made very clear when one scrutinizes the character of this stage from a less romantic point of view. In a sentence: the critique from the side of immorality and license is pretty much without foundation. And hence it is fair to present that critique as masking a different and more thoroughgoing animus. The source of this animus is the delight in Naked Truth: the thing itself, undefiled, unaccoutered, for which the playwright or the vulgar empiric substitute their specious approximations.

[62] For attacks on Sunday playing, see John Field, *Godly Exhortation*, 1583; Nicholas Bownd, *The Doctrine of the Sabbath*, 1595; Stubbes, *Anatomie*, 1583; George Whetstone, *A Touchstone for the Time*, appended to his *mirour for magistrates*, 1584; Norden, *Progress of Piety*, 1596; Lewis Bayly, *Practice of Piety*, 1613; Francis Quarles, *Divine fancies*, 1632; Munday, *Second and third blast*, 1580; Rankins, *A Mirror of Monsters*, 1587; Thomas Brasbridge, *poore mans jewel . . . a treatise of the pestilence*, 1578; John Stockwood, *A sermon preached at Paules Crosse*, 1578.

II   The Naked Truth

THE DELIGHT in the essence, as opposed to the golden veal or stuffed ox of Prometheus, is a legacy to the Renaissance of the primitive Fathers. After all an additional gloss is required, in assessing the total hatred of the stage, as manifest in the early Middle Ages. Augustine —to take him as exemplary—points in his critique to specific abuses. The abuses exist; the indictment goes beyond them. I suppose that Augustine, not less than the reformers of the sixteenth and seventeenth centuries, would have deprecated even a liturgical drama. His more basic objection, like theirs, is to the outwall: art as excrescence. A quotation from the treatise *On Christian Doctrine* is illuminating. The husk which is poetry "shakes sounding pebbles inside its sweet shell, but it is not food for men but for swine."[1] Even the didactic poet, like Hesiod or the makers of the mystery and morality, is committed to this husk. The commitment is provisional; still, the eschatologist or truth-telling man is unwilling to approve it. Like the prophet, he asks implacably: "What hath the straw to do with the wheat?" (Jeremiah, 23:28).

Truth abides beneath the surface, not in the straw or chaff, "not in letters which express words and propositions nor . . . [in] sounds and the pronunciation of

[1] Bk. III, Ch. vii.

sentences." That is Augustine's teacher, Plotinus, who posits in all things the supremacy of disembodied thought. This impalpable activity is congenial to the man of the earlier centuries, not so congenial to the proximate past. Like Orlando in Shakespeare's play, man in the High Middle Ages "can live no longer by thinking." In the Renaissance the ancient impulse to try decapitation recurs. (The phrase is John Crowe Ransom's.) The Renaissance polemicist, as he bears witness to this impulse in formulating his critique of the theatre, goes back—irresistibly, almost unconsciously—to the strictures of the primitive Church.

The reforming zealot—it is Martin Marprelate who stands for him here—opposes himself to the theatre as he is "Tom tell-troth." He cannot "abide to speake . . . by circumloqutions and paraphrases."[2] In this mode of speaking, the playwright is recognized. "For are not their Dialogues puft up with swelling wordes?"[3] But the unwillingness to take the long way around is not peculiar to the dissenter. In his concern for essentiality the Puritan is like the Anglican, and the Protestant, of whatever sect, like the post-Tridentine Catholic. Renaissance man is definable, and different from his predecessors, as he bears out this pervasive concern. John Jewel, the Bishop of Salisbury, in his later years a celebrated apologist for the Anglican establishment, announces proudly that in matters of doctrine, "we have pared every thing away to the very quick."[4] In the

[2] *Reproofe of Martin Junior,* ? 1589, B3.
[3] Crosse, *Vertues Common-wealth,* P2.
[4] Letter of Feb. 1562.

30

theatre this process of refining or coming straight to the
point is reversed. For that reason, the theatre is hateful
to the men of the new dispensation. Typically, the
dramatist works with windlasses and with assays of bias.

I do not mean to pretend that the Elizabethan thea-
tre is blameless. It is not a Puritan but a playwright who
calls playing "the basest trade" (2*Return from Par-
nassus*, IV, iv, 1601). Ben Jonson is of this mind when
(after the fact) he declines to make himself a page "to
that strumpet the Stage."[5] That "shamefull disorder"
could sometimes erupt in the theatre is implied by the
player Dick Tarleton, who entreats "the young people
of the Cittie, either to abstaine altogether from playes,
or at their comming thither to use themselves after a
more quiet order."[6] The unruliness of the audience
leads to the banning of plays under Edward VI in the
private halls of Gray's Inn,[7] and a generation later im-
pels Thomas Twyne, the translator of Virgil, to chide
the Theatre and Curtain for giving rise to bad man-
ners.[8] "Men beside all honesty" are noticed by Tarleton
mingling with the crowd, and making "boote of cloakes,
hats, purses, or what ever they can lay holde on in a
hurley burley." (They are noticed also in St. Paul's.)
Even in the days of performance in the innyards, the
play is evidently an occasion for the "inveygling and al-
leurynge of maides, speciallye orphanes, and good Citi-
zens Children under Age, to prevy and unmete Con-

---

[5] "An Ode: To Himselfe."

[6] *Kind-Harts Dreame* [1592], E4-v. The author is Henry Chet-
tle, who is "quoting" Tarleton's ghost.

[7] Thompson, *Controversy*, p. 3.

[8] *Phisicke against Fortune*, 1579.

tractes.["]9 These lubricious contracts, as they suggest the devil nibbling at our heel, inspire Gosson to address a letter "To the Gentlewomen Citizens of London," and the moralist William Averell to warn young ladies to keep from the playhouse. Ladies lose their reputation there, asserts William Vaughan, the poet and colonizer, who sees nothing amiss in a fugitive and cloistered virtue.[10]

I suppose the trugs and foists and Winchester geese who plied their trade in the Liberties outside the city walls to have resorted to the theatre for business and not pleasure (a nice confounding of Plato's objection). But now on the other hand: "We knowe," says Thomas Leke, a Catholic priest who demurs at his superior's prohibition of the theatre and is instrumental in getting it revoked, "that most of the principal Catholicks about London doe goe to playes."[11] By and large, they are in good company. Real violence becomes conspicuous only after the split between the public and private theatres widens in the reign of Charles I. It is not reserved even then to the plebs.[12] The much-execrated groundlings who stand in the pit are no rabble but a solid amalgam of shopkeepers and craftsmen, educated in

[9] 1574. See "Dramatic Records from the Lansdowne MSS," ed. Chambers and Greg, *Malone Society Collections*, I, Pt. II, 175 (1908: pp. 143-215); and A. Harbage, *Shakespeare's Audience*, p. 74.

[10] Gosson's letter is appended to the *School of Abuse*, 1579. For Averell, see *A Dyall for Dainty Darlings*, 1584; for Vaughan, *The Spirit of Detraction*, 1611. Contemporary accounts of the theatre, mostly hostile, some defensive, are abstracted in Chambers, *Elizabethan Stage*, IV, Appendix C.

[11] Folger MS; Harbage, p. 72.

[12] Bentley, *Shakespeare and His Theatre*, pp. 117-22.

formal ways (as by attendance at a grammar school) as well as Shakespeare presumably was educated.[13] Neither is this audience overwhelmingly masculine. That is the point of the reiterated Warnings to Fair Women. Richard Brathwait acknowledges as he deplores "the usuall resort of Women to Enterludes."[14] It is the observation of a contemporary diarist that "there are always many people and many honorable women in attendance" at the theatre.[15] William Crashaw has got to admit that even "such as will be reputed honest Matrons, nay, the grave men hold it no disgrace to bee there seene and found."[16] On the testimony of the German traveler Thomas Platter, "men and womenfolk visit such places without scruple."[17] Ambassadors to the Court venture more than once to cross over to the Bankside.[18] So does a German nobleman and a Venetian chaplain.

I think they could not have done so had the horrid picture drawn of the theatre by the poet and anagrammatist Francis Lenton been even approximately valid. Lenton is admonishing the well-born and hopefully

[13] Harbage, pp. 64, 60; L. C. Knights, "Education and the Drama in the Age of Shakespeare," *Criterion*, XI (1931-1932), 599-625, and esp. p. 607. E. H. Miller, *Professional Writer in Elizabethan England*, Ch. 2, "The Audience," documents the high level of literacy and the general respect for education among patrons of the theatre. See also P. Sheavyn, *Literary Profession*, pp. 159f.

[14] *English Gentlewoman*, p. 50.

[15] Friedrich Gerschow, one of a party of German travellers, recording in his journal a performance at Blackfriars. See A. M. Nagler, *Shakespeare's Stage*, p. 94.

[16] *Parable of Poison*, p. 24.

[17] 1599; p. 170 in *Thomas Platter's Travels in England*, 1591, trans. Clare Williams, 1937.

[18] Harbage, p. 87.

regenerate playgoer who patronizes "this taperhouse of Sinne." As he taints his ears with bawdy speech and gives himself to idleness, it is "ten to one his Will may breake the fence / Of Reason, and imbrace Concupiscence."[19] But that, in Shakespeare's phrase, is the imposition hereditary ours: the proneness we inherit, simply as we are men. I suppose the conclusion to follow that plays are no more to be included among "the Devils Incarnate of this Age" than the organs of sense which admit them.[20]

This is not to assert that the critic of the stage is disingenuous. It is open to men at any time to blink the fact and lean by preference on the baseless fabric of their vision. But there is more than myopia in the overblown indictment of the Renaissance theatre, as also in the resort by the theatre's opponents to a Biblical injunction, long disused, and the remote fulminations of the primitive Church. "These seem to me," says Mr. Justice Marshall, "the conclusions to which we are conducted by the reason and spirit of the law." And then he adds, "Brother Story will furnish the authorities."

The basic inconsequence of these Renaissance attacks (as also the ulterior motive behind them) is illuminated by the very different nature of the medieval opinion of stage plays, and not least when that opinion is explicitly hostile. Mostly, medieval hostility is directed to specific and ascertainable abuses. Its character is not esthetic or philosophic but practical. What provokes is not the play but the debasing or perhaps the ignoring of the ritual

[19] *The Young Gallants Whirligig*, 1629, p. 18.
[20] Thomas Lodge in *Wits Miserie*, 1596, p. 40.

out of which the play emerges.[21] Early in the fifteenth
century, a Minorite friar seeks to postpone the pageant
cycle at York to the day after Corpus Christi, to insure
undivided attention to the religious service and proces-
sion on the day of the feast.[22] But this friar does not
deprecate playing per se. In his sermons he commends
the York pageant as good intrinsically and very worthy
of performance. It seems to him neither criminal nor
offensive to God to ascend to the better by way of the
good. Aquinas sanctions the profession of the *histrio* or
stage player, so long as he refrains from indecorous
behavior.[23] Langland withholds his sanction, but on the
same contingent grounds: the player is a "jangler" or
buffoon. The Church, which seeks insistently to narrow
the appeal of the decadent theatre of Rome, permits a
different kind of drama to transfer from the Mass to
Matins, and so to find greater favor and enjoy greater
scope. On the conviction that this scope is overweening
—a provisional criticism—hostility to the drama de-
pends. *Audire Verbum Dei*: that is the greater impera-
tive, says a Dominican theologian, in complaining of
miracula as keeping the people from sermons.[24] Even so
late as the second half of the sixteenth century, the Gen-
eral Assembly of the Scottish Kirk, in forbidding the
dramatic representation of sacred events, does not dis-

---

[21] H. S. Symmes, *Les Débuts de la Critique Dramatique en Angle-
terre*, pp. 6-12.

[22] William Melton in 1426.

[23] See M. Barras, *Stage Controversy in France*, pp. 23f.

[24] John de Bromyarde, *Summa Praedicantium*, *c*.1360, pub.
1485.

countenance playing but only such shows as make for "contempt and profanation."[25]

From time to time throughout the Middle Ages, the participation of the clergy in dramatic activity engenders protest. But this recurrent protest, whether it is urged by individual reformers or codified by the Church in Council, is not directed to the thing itself. It is directed to intemperate behavior in church, or wherever the crowd comes together, or to a tampering with or diluting of the service. In this matter of the mysteries and miracles, the clergy and the laity see eye to eye.[26] As the drama quits the church, protest subsides—or else its tenor changes. Root and branch hostility arises only with the coming of the Renaissance. It is in this period that more lofty considerations begin to supervene.

The term "Renaissance" is so inclusive as, potentially, to mean everything and nothing. I employ it in this connection to skirt what seems to me the greater danger of exclusiveness, as when one identifies with the Reformation in religious dogma the rising hostility to the stage. The reformer is, indifferently, Protestant or Catholic— or irenicist or skeptic, like Bacon, Hobbes, or Sprat. The attack in which he participates is not occasioned by a change in modes of worshiping the deity—except as this change is itself emblematic of a radical alteration in the perceiving and understanding of the world without the self. Descartes the Catholic philosopher, as he denies the reality of particular forms, is of the Renaissance; so are Zwingli and Tyndale, as they repudiate the doctrine of transubstantiation; or Galileo, as he reads the uni-

[25] 1575; Craig, *English Religious Drama*, p. 354.
[26] Craig, pp. 89, 92f.

verse under the aspect of mathematical design. *Nuda veritas*: in each case it is the impulse to essentiality that governs. In point of this common impulse, Reformation and Counter-Reformation are to be described as similar manifestations of a state of mind or psychology, pervasive in the time in which either is accomplished.

Considerations of the primary truth do not occur to the twelfth-century prelate who reproves the monks of Augsburg for absenting themselves from their refectory, failing the performance there of a theatrical entertainment like the story of Herod;[27] or to that Abbess of Clerkenwell, a hundred years later, who complains to the King that her crops are trampled by the crowds attending miracle plays and wrestling matches in the open fields. That is a reasonable complaint, and it informs the distinction drawn by the Anglo-Norman poet William of Waddington between playing out of doors and those more seemly rituals performed in the church itself. Clerics, says William, "may make a representation"—than which nothing is more hateful to the Renaissance draconian—"if it is done modestly in the office of Holy Church . . . of how Jesus Christ, the Son of God, was laid in the sepulchre, and of the Resurrection, for the sake of greater devoutness. But if they make foolish assemblies in city streets or in graveyards after meals, when fools are glad to come . . . it is [not] done for the honour of God, but rather in truth for that of the devil."[28] Robert Mannyng of Brunne, who renders William's treatise in English, appears to affirm this dis-

[27] Gerhoh of Reichersberg, in Craig, pp. 90f.
[28] *Manuel des Pechiez*, c.1300, trans. E. K. Chambers, *English Literature at the Close of the Middle Ages*, p. 13.

37

tinction. Miracles which adulterate their sacred purpose, as by masking and mumming, are forbidden by decree. But the church drama of the Resurrection is not forbidden. Neither is the Nativity story:

> And he may pleye, withouten plight,
> How God was bore in Yule night.[29]

The decree of which the poet takes notice dates from the previous century and is the work of Pope Innocent III. In a letter deprecating the boisterous excesses of the Feast of Fools at Christmas, Innocent forbids the "theatrical" employing of masks in the church service.[30] Gregory IX, in the next generation, has these excesses in mind (Decretals of 1227-1241). So does John of Salisbury, than whom no more equable a man ever lived, in attacking what he calls *tota joculatorum scena*. It is the intrusion of buffoonery in sacred business that a twelfth-century abbot objects to, in seeking to abolish histrionic gestures—but not as they are mimetic; rather as they are incongruous.[31] When, in the middle of the thirteenth century, Robert Grosseteste, the Chancellor of Oxford and Bishop of Lincoln, instructs his archdeacons to put a stop to performances of miracle plays by the clergy, it is because they are not the plays they purport to be, but drinking bouts and seasonal revels. The point is pragmatic. It is, for example, the boast of a good friar—in a fourteenth-century poem attacking the mendicant orders—that he and his fellows are no haunters of taverns or fairs—or miracle plays.[32]

---

[29] *Handlynge Synne*, 1304, ll. 4647-48; Craig, p. 91.
[30] 1207; Chambers, *English Literature*, p. 14.
[31] Aelred of Rievaulx.
[32] *Piers Plowman's Crede*, 1394.

This unlucky conjunction is difficult to annul. A century after Grosseteste lays down the law, plays are still performed at Lincoln; the crowds that flock to see them are still behaving in the old unruly way.[33] It is, however, not the playing that rubs but the disorder. Or it is the vulgarizing of a noble theme. I think that much is clear from the very particular praise accorded the drama in London by William Fitzstephen (d.? 1190), the biographer of St. Thomas à Becket. There are, on the one hand, those "theatrical spectacles and stage plays" which are religious only by courtesy, in the way of a perfunctory genuflection now and then. It is *"Laus Deo"* and on with the show. And then there are, what Fitzstephen approves: "holy dramas, representations of miracles that holy confessors have wrought or the representations of the sufferings that the constancy of martyrs have illuminated."[34]

Fitzstephen, who confers this qualified approval in the second half of the twelfth century, typifies the medieval attitude toward the drama. Four centuries later, and in a more secular age, the provisional tolerance he bestows on the dramatic representation of reality is denied. But the medieval period is ascetic, and the Renaissance dedicated to the body and its claims? In the later age, physical reality is everywhere attested: on stage, in pictorial art and especially in portraiture, in sculpture, in the celebration of the nude. It is, however, in the Renaissance, and not the Middle Ages, that the artist,

[33] According to William Courtney, Archbishop of Canterbury, commenting on a visit to the city.

[34] Craig, p. 102.

who venerates the surface, is driven from the common-wealth.

The victory of Savonarola is impermanent; so is the Rule of the Saints under Cromwell. But the eccentric character of these fanatic events diverts the understanding from what is normative or typical about them. Neither is sensational, except on the surface. Each connects to an abiding strain in the spirit or temperament of the Renaissance. Cromwell, for whom the mind is the man, is not the antithesis of Milton, the sensuous poet; nor is Bacon the scientist to be set against Ben Jonson or Christopher Marlowe. One may say that Chaucer has his natural complement in the mathematical philosophers who follow William of Ockham. This is only to say that all ages are various, in respect of the men who compose them. But Chaucer in his psychology differs conclusively from the mathematicians, and even though he is the author of a treatise on the astrolabe. In the Renaissance, conversely, the preoccupation with abstract truth and, concurrently, a disdain for the concrete exemplification, is conspicuous along the entire spectrum. Milton and Cromwell stand, philosophically, on the same ground. Though Marlowe and Jonson vindicate humanity as they represent it on stage, neither offers to delineate an indigenous man. Bacon the lawgiver, who is largely indifferent to empirical studies, is their contemporary in more than chronological ways.

The cultivator of the primary truth, who is everywhere to be encountered in the sixteenth and seventeenth centuries, is powerfully influential in determining the bias and direction of his age. He cannot endure the representation of a real presence: what the Cambridge

Platonist John Smith stigmatizes as "the filth and un-
clean tinctures of corporeity." Like the unhistorical
Jesus, as imagined by Bishop John Bale, he has only con-
tempt for cope, cross, or candlestick, or ashes or palms,
or the holy bread and water. Dumb ceremonies seem to
him the leaven of the Pharisees. Mitres, tippets, furred
amises and shaven crowns, he lumps together as beg-
garly shadows. To worship in outward things is, if he
has his way, forbidden by the secular arm. An old-
fashioned opponent is right in imputing to him the de-
sire that "all the gates of our senses and ways to man's
understanding should be shut up."[35] Partaking of the
Eucharist is a sensuous way to understanding. Accord-
ingly, and by edict of Parliament, every officeholder
must declare his belief "that there is not any transub-
stantiation in the sacrament of the Lord's Supper" (Test
Act of 1673).

Concurrent with this hatred of corporeity, explicable
in terms of it, a thorough-going hatred of the drama
begins to be perceptible, after so many centuries of rela-
tive tolerance and even approbation. Carnality describes
the miracle play not less than the secular drama. In con-
sequence, "all scurrilous and rattlebrained Players," and
even those who play "the passion of Christ . . . upon a
scaffold," begin to weigh equally as they "fill the rude
peoples heads with vanitie." The wickedness of this of-
fice is attested in the savagery with which it is paid
home. To satisfy the demands of mimesis, "hee that . . .
[is] crucified for Christ" must bear, like the little boy

[35] M. M. Knappen, *Tudor Puritanism*, pp. 66-68. Bale's opponent
is Bishop Stephen Gardiner. For attacks on the theatre as "carnal"
(superficial), see J. Barish, "Exhibitionism and the Anti-Theatrical
Prejudice," *ELH*, xxxvi (1969), 4-9.

in *Cambises*, "a bladder of blood at his side." (The chronicler is Edmund Rudierde, who is remembering a performance of the Passion Play.) And now the melodramatic requital. It is into the bladder that "another player should have thrust his speare, but the weapon hit upon the false Christs side, and slew him, by the fall of whom, another that played the part of a woman lamenting by the Crosse, was also slaine, and his brother that was first slaine, slew him that slew his brother, and so was hanged worthely for his labour."[36] That is "a worthy spectacle" to the truth-telling man, who sees no reason to distinguish "holy dramas" from "theatrical spectacles and stage plays."

Already, in the later Middle Ages, this saving distinction ceases to apply. The denunciation of plays prepared by a fifteenth-century Dean of the Faculty of Theology at Paris no longer discriminates between kinds: playing is anathema, irrespective of its subject or ostensible purpose.

> Who, I ask you, with any Christian feelings, will not condemn when priests and clerks are seen . . . running and leaping about the whole church in unblushing shameless iniquity . . . [or] driving about the town and its theatres in carts and deplorable carriages to make an infamous spectacle.[37]

In the closing years of the fourteenth century, a Wyclifite *Treatise of miraclis pleyinge* discovers impiety simply in the fact of mimesis. "As this feyned recreacioun of pleyinge of miraclis is fals conceite," so is it

[36] *Thunderbolt*, p. 39.
[37] Letter of 1445; A. P. Rossiter, *English Drama from Early Times*, p. 59.

to be contemned as "double shrewidnesse." What the preacher requires is a kind of abstract art, which is ideally no art at all, "but as nakid lettris to a clerk to reden the treuthe." Now the argument of the medieval writer is rejected, that plays are agreeable as they "make men be in beleve gode"; as well as the more timorous suggestion that men, as they are frail, must enjoy themselves a little, and better "by pleyinge of miraclis than by pleyinge of other japis."[38] Wyclif is absolute in condemning "vein playes." But the adjective is understood as redundant. That is why the Council of Basle (1435) bans not only the mock-religious Feast of Fools but entertainments of whatever nature in the church or churchyard.

It is out of the Mass, early in the ninth century, that the modern drama first emerges. In the fifteenth century, paternity is disavowed. A century later, Edmund Bonner, the Bishop of London, commands the clergy of his diocese to prohibit in their churches and chapels "all manner of common plays, games, or interludes" (1542). Bonner is an ardent Catholic. Northbrooke, who deprecates the performing of interludes as they "mingle scurrilitie with Divinitie,"[39] is of the Protestant party. But Catholic and Protestant, in their judgment of stage plays, are the same.

This total condemnation is right and apposite in time. I see it as auguring, like the resurgence of mysticism in the later Middle Ages, the dawn of a new Platonism. *Universalia ante rem*: it is the lust for the primary as

---

[38] *Handlynge Synne*, 1. 4645; Chambers, *English Literature*, p. 14. For the attack on mimesis, see J. Barish, "The Antitheatrical Prejudice," *Critical Quarterly*, VIII (1966), 329-48.

[39] *Treatise*, p. 32.

against the secondary truth that dictates the new and sweeping hatred of plays as plays.

Medieval man is devoted to the manifold tracings of the surface; the more exclusive impulse that defines his successor is to strike through the mask. As the more ample world of the Middle Ages goes down, commitment to the one truth that saves and recures becomes overmastering. Now vagaries of spirit are not to be entertained; neither are vagaries of intellect. That is why Luther so shockingly denounces man's reason as "the devil's bride, the beautiful whore" which Faith, as it is zealous of knowing "nothing but the word of God," must "trample under foot." Reason is a curb to the undivided pursuit of our purpose, which is to know the Truth that makes us free. But how do we know this Truth, unless by intuition? And hence the fanatic proposition: "Whoever wants to be a Christian should tear the eyes out of his reason." Among the Lutherans, philosophy has no value; that is a Roman Catholic jibe.[40] But the men of the new dispensation (who are as often to be found on the Catholic as on the Protestant side) do not turn it aside but endorse it. They are mindful of St. Paul's advice to the Colossians not to let any man spoil them by philosophy. According to Luther, who is speaking on this head for fellow reformers like Martin Bucer and Zwingli and Peter Martyr, one cannot be proficient in Aristotle and Christ.

It is Tertullian come to life again, after a thousand years: "*Quid ergo Athenis et Hierosolymis? Quid*

---

[40] *Nullo apud Lutheranos philosophiam esse in pretio. Tischreden,* XII, 1530; III, 215; V, 425; *Works,* 1959, ed. Pelikan and Lehmann, CI, 374.

Academiae et Ecclesiae?"[41] We are here as on a field
of battle. Philosophy, mincing poetry: whatever is felt
as accouterment, only beguiles us from our business.
The proposition is tenable even of the greatest art. The
serious drama of Calderón is intrinsically religious. In
the seventeenth century that is not enough to clear it
from reproach. Calderón, as his piety waxes, conceives
of the stage as beguiling. Following his ordination to
the priesthood, he turns from the writing of plays as
labor done to no ultimate purpose.[42] Ben Jonson, as the
eschatological fervor grows upon him, laments with
horror "that he had profaned the Scripture, in his
plays."[43] Corneille and Racine, in the seventeenth cen-
tury, are infinitely greater than Gosson and Anthony
Munday and John Lyly in the sixteenth. They have this
in common: each is a playwright, and each, as the con-
viction takes him of man's fallen nature, contemns the
stage and directs his mind to last things. "I will cast
my wits in a new mould," Lyly announces, "for I find it
folly that one foot being in the grave, I should have
the other on the stage" (1597). It is not a wooden scaf-
fold but "the World" that is "our Stage, our Life an
Act . . . Without Vertue, all humaine glory is a fading
beauty."[44]

The eschatologist endorses the spirit of Pascal's in-
junction: *Chercher en gémissant.* Our business is not to
delight nor be delighted; it is to seek with groaning.

[41] *De Praescr.* 7; quoted in Farrar, p. 183n.
[42] Calderón, who ceases to write in 1651, begins again only on
the importuning of the King.
[43] M. Chute, *Ben Jonson*, p. 372, quoting George Morley.
[44] Brathwait, *English Gentlewoman*, **1v.

"Habit of the stage, relic of the Amorite, imitation of AntiChrist": these are the tremendous terms which a Calvinist like Theodore Beza reserves for the chorister's surplice.[45] It is on the hill of Vézelay that Beza, the image breaker, is born in 1519. The great sculptures of the narthex, in that noblest of all Romanesque churches, are to him as flat and tedious as the songs of the poets to the Jacobean entrepreneur. *Quid dant artes?* In winning to the one goal, what does not help us hinders. That is why Lenin, who belongs with the great simplifiers like Calvin and Gregory the Great, confesses to Gorki that though he loves the Appassionata of Beethoven, he will close his ears against it.

"Will the Latin grammar save an immortal soul?" That is Pope Gregory, whose scornful question is felt as answering itself. Radical Protestantism, as it finds the answer congenial, confesses its real affinity to the earlier Church. God, as Luther presents him, "does not speak grammatical vocables, but true essential things."[46] The pagan drama is dead; the Elizabethan drama is not really its avatar: still the polemicists of the sixteenth and seventeenth centuries return insistently to the primitive Fathers. That is because each is intoxicated with millenarian fervor, and concurrently and sequentially, with the impulse to volatilize the surface of things. *"Externa variant, interna manent."* Luther, who formulates this opposition between the husk and the kernel, is unwilling to cast himself in the role of an innovator. "We are all unconscious Hussites," he remarks. "Paul

---

[45] Quoted in C. D. Bowen, *The Lion and the Throne*, p. 54.
[46] Quoted in Farrar, p. 340.

and Augustine are Hussites to the letter."[47] I think he is right.

"This world is in haste and approaches its end": the medieval prelate Wulfstan, dilating on the horrors of an earlier age,[48] differs from his successors in the modern period as he indulges despair. But these successors, if they are more sanguine, are not less convinced that the day of reckoning is at hand. This conviction is anguished and insistent in the writings of the Fathers. What follows is a drastic narrowing of the old and thoughtless commitment to superficies. The reading of pagan authors is forbidden, as by the Council of Carthage (398). "What hath Horace to do with the Psalter?" asks St. Jerome. Even theological speculation is rejected, as it is involved with the excogitation of words. An early commentator on the Apocalypse is uneasily aware that "this is no time to discuss Scripture."[49] It is written of an ancient hermit that "his life went by in a great silence." What is there to talk about? That is the implication in the crazed and lovely saying of the desert monk who addresses St. Anthony: "Tell me, I pray thee, how fares the human race: if new roofs be risen in the ancient cities, whose empire is it that now sways the world." Jerome in the fourth century tells of seeing monks in the Syrian desert, "one of whom lived a recluse for thirty years, on barley bread and muddy water: another [who] in an ancient well . . . kept himself in life on five dry figs a day."[50]

---

[47] Farrar, pp. 334n., 312 (quoting a letter of 1520).
[48] *Sermo Lupi ad Anglos*, 1014.
[49] Farrar, p. 247.
[50] Waddell, pp. 45 (quoting *Historia Monachorum*), 35, 32.

But this life of abstention and rejection,

Emptying the sensual with deprivation
Cleansing affection from the temporal

is more rich than deprived. I quote from the *Collationes* of John Cassian of Marseilles (*c.* 360-435), who is among the founders of monasticism:

> And so he who keeps an anxious watch over the purity of the inner man will seek those places which have no rich fertility to seduce his mind to their tilling, nor beguile him from his fixed and motionless abiding in his cell to work that is done under the sky, whereby his thoughts are emptied out in the open, and all direction of the mind and that keen vision of its goal are scattered over diverse things.

The goal changes, then and now; but the abhorrence of scattering or of flying from the center is constant; "and this can be avoided by no man, however anxious and vigilant, save he that shuts in soul and body together within the fence of his walls." Now what this fence encloses is to be scrutinized more jealously than ever before:

> Like a mighty fisherman, in the apostle's fashion, perceiving his food in the depths of his most quiet heart, intent and motionless he catches the swimming shoal of his thoughts: and gazing curiously into the depths as from an upstanding rock, judges what fish a man may wholesomely draw in, and which he may pass by . . . .[51]

The fertile matter of art, as it seduces the mind to its tilling, is conceived as a scattering or diversion. "And again," says the anchorite, "for the pipe and lyre and

[51] Cassian is quoting the Abbot Abraham, in Waddell, pp. 160f.

other kinds of music wherein I delighted at my feasts, I say to myself twelve psalms by day, and twelve by night."[52] Gregory the Great, as it is his purpose to evacuate the world of sense and fancy, makes ignorance a virtue. Knowing no literature, he will enter into the power of the Lord.[53] What galls him even more than the benighted practice of the heathen—as Gibbon remembers enthusiastically—is "the profane learning of a bishop, who taught the art of grammar, studied the Latin poets, and pronounced with the same voice the praises of Jupiter and those of Christ."[54] Gregory scorns "to observe all art of style, in which pupils are drilled in schools of the outer training," and despises "a conformity to constructions and moods and cases of prepositions." (He is a very difficult writer.) As he believes it unworthy "to subjugate the words of the Heavenly Oracle to the rules of Donatus" the grammarian, he "can scarcely mention without shame," when writing to Desiderius, the Archbishop of Vienne, "that your fraternity explains grammar to certain persons. What a deadly and heinous fault!"

But apparently all learning is under ban, as excrescent: King Alfred is not aware of a single monk south of the Thames who can translate the Breviary.[55] Painted poetry, on the other hand, as it is wholly gratuitous, is not without its devotees. *Quid Inieldus Christo?* asks the scholarly Alcuin (*c.* 735-804), embittered at this preferring of pleasure to profit. What have the songs of

[52] *Verba Seniorum*, x, lxxvi; Waddell, p. 106.
[53] *Quoniam non cognovi litteraturam introibo in potentias Domini.* W. P. Ker, *The Dark Ages*, p. 25, cites Psalm lxx.15.
[54] *Decline and Fall*, Ch. xlv.
[55] Farrar, p. 246, and note.

49

Ingeld, the pagan hero, to do with Christ? But Alcuin is the chief begetter of the Carolingian Renaissance. Evidently the truth that is to rise again, in this redintegrating of the knowledge of the past, is not the partial truth of the poet.

In the opening of his life of St. Benedict, Pope Gregory heaps contempt on all literary study. Learned ignorance, the possession of the man who is "wisely ignorant and wisely untaught," is pitted against the superficial learning which is the business of art.[56] The Renaissance is adumbrated. Petrarch, dilating *On his own ignorance*; or Joseph Glanvill in the seventeenth century, asserting the *Vanity of Dogmatizing*; or Nicholas of Cusa, two hundred years earlier, propounding his *docta ignorantia*: each of these writers—who, among them, encompass the whole of the Renaissance—is animated, like the Fathers, by a common will to put away superficies and to achieve the thing itself. Boethius, writing in the same century as Gregory the Great, sees art under this aspect of superficies. When Philosophy finds him in the company of the Muses, he allows her to deride them as tragical harlots (*scenicas meretriculas*) who kill the crop with fruitless thorns.[57] The Venerable Bede (?673-735), "a man whom it is easier to admire than to extol," poises on the one hand the work of Homer, Virgil, and Lucretius and, on the other "our dramas": the Song of Solomon, Ecclesiastes, and Job.[58] His preference is not

[56] *Scienter nesciens, et sapienter indoctus*, in *Dialogues*, ii, Pref.; Ker, p. 92.

[57] *Consolation of Philosophy*, I.i.

[58] The characterization of Bede is from William of Malmesbury, quoted in Farrar, p. 248; Bede expresses his preference in *De Arte Metrica*, quoted in Ker, p. 25n.

in doubt. Scripture makes for our salvation; profane poetry, as it is not so gravid, makes only for a specious entertainment. It is not because he is given to self-mortification that Bede eschews the one for the other. Like Plato he knows what it means really to love oneself.

What benefit is there to posterity, asks Sulpicius Severus (c. 365-c. 420), the ecclesiastical historian, in the legends of Hector's valor? But the question is rhetorical. *Ars longa, vita brevis*; and therefore let art be put down.

III The Thief of Time

THIS MORE alert eye to our benefit is necessarily more
exclusive. It does not look with much favor on the lilies
of the field, in whom the artist is figured. The artist, as
he neither toils nor spins, makes little for our benefit.
Like that prattling daughter of Pan whom Sir Francis
Bacon describes, he fills the world "with idle tales; be-
ing ever barren, empty, and servile."[1] The Puritan fore-
bears of Nathaniel Hawthorne think it sufficient retribu-
tion for their sins that the family tree should bear an
idler as its topmost bough. They want to know what
kind of useful business is involved in the writing of
stories: "what mode of glorifying God, or being service-
able to mankind in his day and generation."[2] As he
takes the point, Hawthorne is mute. *Quid dant artes?*

This hostile question is uttered first by a twelfth-
century poet, who is applying for a benefice and under-
stands on which side his bread is buttered. It is implicit
in the writings of the Fathers. Chrysostom castigates
stage plays as they are productive of "fornication, in-
temperance, and every kind of impurity"; but also for
the idleness and extravagance they engender: for the
"waste of time [and] useless spending of days" and the
squandering of money on harlots and the omitting of

[1] *Advancement of Learning*, Bk. II, Ch. xiii.
[2] "The Custom House," in preface to *The Scarlet Letter*.

"not a few of . . . [one's] domestic concerns for the sake of this unseasonable employment."[3] Time runs in the theatre, and money is time; and man by definition or prescription is not to be prodigal of either. Man is born to pray and save.

But this more strict surveillance of the credentials of art is, until the Renaissance, not so typical as portentous. It is "a baby figure of the mass of things to come." For not until the Renaissance unlocks the wealth of new continents and creates in the process a new mercantile class, not until there dawns an age of economic expansion and fluidity in which it is open to the last to be first, does the equation of time and money become greatly apparent or its implications greatly pressing. The shift to mercantile enterprise and mercantile values; simultaneously, the contempt for a less palpable kind of activity and the devaluing of its product: these turn, first of all, on the greater accrual that results from the pursuit of material gain.

To assert a connection between this pursuit and the new and slighting estimation of art is not to stipulate, for the war against poetry, an etiology that is narrowly materialistic. The polemical literature of the period demonstrates conclusively the existence of an economic motive in the attack on poetry and plays. But the meanly selfish bias of the entrepreneur differs in degree—so much so as almost to constitute a difference in kind—from the impersonal vision of the new philosopher, who wishes to "gather from the whole store of things" what-

[3] Homily xv, "Concerning the Statues," *Ante-Nicene Fathers*, ix, 442; xlii, "The Acts of the Apostles," xi, 262; lxvi, "The Gospel of St. Matthew," x, 407; i, "St. Matthew," x, 7.

ever makes "most for the uses of life."[4] The intention
or motivation is in each case "economic"—in Bacon and
Colbert, as in the vulgar money-lender like Bess of
Hardwick or Horatio Palavincino. This means that eco-
nomics, as I invoke it here, is a portmanteau term, and
fruitful of a wide range of definitions. Or it is, to quote
Ralegh in his *History of the World*, a coffer with a
double bottom, which men, when they peruse, "see not
all that . . . [it holds] on the sudden and at once" (v,
iii, 1). To seek to encompass the different holdings of
this coffer is to treat necessarily of the attack on poetry
from the side of morality, and metaphysics, and not
least of self-aggrandizement.

The economic motive, narrowly defined—as in the
career of Sir Giles Overreach, adumbrating Max Weber
—is very powerful in the second half of the sixteenth
century. It is in this period that the joint-stock enter-
prise, that hallmark of all subsequent times, begins to
flourish. The wealthy merchants who ensinew the Le-
vant Company (incorporated in 1581) realize, in its
early years, a trebling of their investment.[5] *Quid dant
artes?* But aggrandizement is not contingent on great
wealth. If a shareholder of modest means can expect a
return of 87 1/2%, as from the first joint-stock voyage
of the East India Company; if so much can be pressed
from so little, it is not hard to understand why the
amassing of this little becomes a point of honor. Neither
is it hard to grasp the new and critical importance of
time, after long centuries sublimely indifferent to it.

---

[4] Bacon in the *Advancement*; quoted in Loren Eiseley, *Francis
Bacon and the Modern Dilemma*, p. 23.

[5] P. Ramsey, *Tudor Economic Problems*, p. 71.

"Our rest we expect elsewhere," says Oliver Cromwell, in a greatly mordant phrase; "that will be durable."[6]

In the more dramatic good fortune of Sir Francis Drake and those who assist him in fitting out the *Golden Hind* on its epic voyage, the indolence of a thousand years receives its quietus. Having completed his circumnavigation of the globe (1580), Drake returns to England with enough bullion, jewels, spice, and silk to pay to each of his shareholders a dividend of 1,700%. But this voyage is even more rich in implication: money, in the tremendous apophthegm of Volpone, has become "the world's soul."

In the sixteenth century the proper use of time is the prosecuting of virtuous business, which one will gloss as his bias directs him.

> Wherefore in time let us arise,
> And slouthfulness doo cleane away!
> Doing some godly exercise
> As servantes true while it is day.[7]

That is how the moralist sees it. It is possible to define this exercise more concretely. A sixteenth-century writer, repelled by the eagerness with which his contemporaries chase the profits of the Netherlands trade, remarks that "if Englishmen's fathers were hanged in Antwerp's gate, their children would creep betwixt their legs to come into the . . . town."[8] This is not to comment on their folly but on their acumen. There is something to be said for niggarding and creeping. The end crowns the work and approves it.

[6] Letter to St. John, 1648.
[7] *Court of Virtue*, Y8.   [8] Ramsey, p. 9.

The exercise which is art entails, on the other hand, the "supporting of a great sorte of idle lubbers and buzzing Dronets to sucke up and devoure the good Honey."[9] That is what the players do: they "sucke up the bottomes of . . . young Prodigals superfluities, to whome they stick as fast as a kibe to a Boyes heele."[10] The theatre works the ruin of industrious men, who "leave their honest callings, live idlely, and gadde to those places where the divel displayeth his banner."[11] This ruin has its social and pecuniary aspects. As "young gentlemen by wilde unthriftinesse become sports to Theators . . . [they] cannot sit on their Fathers seates to do good in the Common-wealth."[12] Dick Tarleton, the comic actor, is amusing on this head. "Fie upon following playes," he cries with a show of indignation, "the expence is wondrous." Tarleton sees what is at stake, as in affecting to lament "that a man should spende his two pence on . . . [plays] in an after-noone [and] heare covetousnes amongst them daily quipt at, being one of the commonest occupations in the countrey."[13]

It is this occupation that rationalizes the ascent of the taverner's son Francesco Datini (1335-1410), whose statue, which still stands in the square of his native city of Prato, represents him as holding not a nosegay of verses but a sheaf of bills of exchange. *Nil penna, sed usus*: ignore the plumage; look to the practical value. That is the counsel the emblem writer (for example,

[9] Stubbes, *Anatomie of Abuses*, N5v.
[10] *This Worlds Folly*, B3.
[11] *Vertues Common-wealth*, Q1v.
[12] Thomas Adams, *The Gallants Burden*, 1612, p. 16.
[13] *Kind-Harts Dreame*, E2v-3.

56

Geoffrey Whitney) dins into the ears of nouveaux riches like Thomas Deloney's hero, Jack of Newberry, or those who aspire to riches, like Thomas Dekker's hero, Simon Eyre.[14] In the career of Sir Thomas Smith, a beggarly scholar at Cambridge (and subsequently Vice Chancellor to the University) whose father keeps the local almshouse in the little town of Walden, the fruit of the dedication to material gain is vividly apparent.

> Raise up therefore thy lazy limbes,
> apply thy minde to paine,
> Both foode and cloath and all things else,
> with ease thou shalt attaine.[15]

That is the new or applied morality. Henry Crosse, as he affirms it, discovers in "idlenesse the roote of all evill."[16] He means it is subversive of application and so of attaining. When it really avails to add the halfpence to the pence, then the muted praise of thrift and labor becomes a paean of praise and the unthrift is loaded with contempt. That is why, in the polemical literature of the sixteenth and seventeenth centuries, the argument is urged with such hectic insistence that plays are wicked because they are wasteful.[17]

The translator Sir Thomas North, who asks us (in the *Dial of Princes*, 1557) to keep from the play, offers essentially the frugal reasons put forward long ago in

[14] *Choice of Emblemes*, 1586, G2.
[15] *Vertues Common-wealth*, O4.
[16] S3v.
[17] For the deprecating of idleness, and the insistence on the sanctity of time, see C. and K. George, *Protestant Mind of the English Reformation*, pp. 133f.

57

the homilies of Chrysostom. But they have new content now. This content describes the railings of Thomas Lupton, a vendor of recipes and nostrums, to whom it is imprudent that men should "spende the time vainely, and consume their money fondely."[18] Wickedness is not much worse than indiscretion: John Donne in his *Anniversaries* (l. 338). "The time present is our onely time," says the Rev. Robert Bolton of Brasenose College, Oxford. (One remembers Friar Bacon, another fellow in that college, who forbore to seize the time and lost his opportunity forever.) Modern man broods incessantly on this melancholy truth, that "wee have no more power and command over the time to come, than over the time past."[19] The fleeting moment is decisive. "Time is short . . . Time is precious."[20] As that is so, it behooves us to choose our recreations with an eye to "little cost, least losse of time."[21] John Webster, a clerical supporter of the new science, desires "above all other things . . . that time be not mispent, or trifled away." Loss of time is "irreparable . . . and utterly irrevocable, and therefore . . . long vacations, relaxations and intermissions are to be looked upon as *Scylla* and *Charibdis*, the rocks and shelves whereon young men may easily suffer Shipwrack."[22] Thomas Heywood's puritanical antagonist labors this point in chastising the "spend-all Gentlemen" who "passe away . . . the most precious time of their life" to "maintain a great sort of idle and

[18] *Siuqila*, 1580, p. 27.
[19] *Some Generall Directions for a Comfortable Walking with God,* 1625, p. 161.
[20] Pp. 158f.
[21] Hill, *Pathway to Prayer*, R7.
[22] *Academiarum Examen*, 1654, Ch. xi.

buzzing drones" (the reprise is significant), and to an end that is "fruitlesse, without any profite."[23] Even the condemned criminal laments with his latest breath the "flitting time" he has devoted "to the Theatre and Curtaine." This insight after the fact, imputed to the conspirator Anthony Babington, comes too late to save him from the gallows.

"Trouble and toyle draw us to life, ease & idelnesses bring destruction": that is the first principle, according to Gosson.[24] And now the corollary: plays "nourish Idlenesse . . . [which] is the Mother of Vice."[25] It is, however, more pertinent to indict them not as they are vicious but as they "are prejudiciall and unprofitable to the common wealth," or else as those who patronize plays "consume many Patrimonies, yearely spending many poundes on these vaine representations."[26] Gosson also inveighs against playwrights as "utter enimies to vertue," and players as "the Sonnes of idlenesse." That is as he has found them "unprofitable members." The plays which they fabricate, like "Common Bowling Allyes, are privy Mothes, that eate uppe the credite of many idle Citizens: whose gaines at home, are not able to weighe down their losses abroad."[27] The chief count against the player and playwright is that they "juggle in good earnest the money out of other mens purses into their owne handes."[28]

<hr>

[23] I. G., *Refutation of the Apology for Actors*, 1615, A3, H4v. The second quotation repeats Stubbes in *Anatomie*, N5v.

[24] *School of Abuse*, L8v.

[25] *Refutation*, H3v.   [26] II, A3v.

[27] *School of Abuse*, G8v, A3, D4.

[28] Munday, *Second and third blast of retrait from plaies and Theatres*, 1580.

In the theatre, men present themselves as women. John Rainolds, Gosson's old tutor at Oxford, is very sore on this point. But what exacerbates his displeasure is the neglect of business that accompanies that odious representation. The first item in his indictment of "the vanitie of apparell," as flaunted by "the plagues of stageplayers," is "idlenes, a sweete evill." He desires the destruction of "those wanton lusts" which the players epitomize as they are "unhonest"—but also as they "draw men from studies."[29]

At a performance before the Queen of Richard Edwardes' *Palamon and Arcite*, a rich cloak is contributed to the funeral pyre which burns for the knightly hero, who wins the battle and loses the lady and his life. To one of the spectators, who "would have stayed [the player] by the arm with an oath," this extravagance is not to be borne. The Queen, like the player, is more easy. "Go, fool!" she says to the provident man, "he knoweth his part."[30] It is a hateful part to the clergyman William Ames, who is poignantly aware of the waste entailed by plays. The formal ground of his attack on the drama is moral; that is the rite he is committed to perform. His greatest spleen is reserved, however, to the dissipating of money in the playhouse.[31]

[29] *Six Conclusions*, p. 678. Rainolds, in a letter to Dr. Thomas Thornton of Christ Church, Oxford, Feb. 6, 1591/2, emphasizes the waste of time and money occasioned by plays; and again, replying to William Gager, July 31, 1592. See Young, *Transactions*, pp. 594, 601, 603, notes to 631-33. J. W. Binns of the University of Birmingham has in progress an edtion of the works of William Gager, with translation and commentary, and including documents relating to the Gager–Rainolds controversy.

[30] G. K. Hunter, *John Lyly*, p. 112.

[31] *Cases of Conscience*, ? 1643, Bk. v, Ch. xxxix, "Of immodest luxury."

The interpenetrating of real and ostensible reasons is already apparent in the first full-length indictment of *Vaine plaies or Enterludes* (1579). Lustful behavior is conspicuous among the author's accusations; but that is not why he demands of the players that they "become true labourers in the Common wealth . . . [and] gette their own livinges with their owne handes, in the sweate of their face."[32] The demand is not much honored. As the seventeenth century opens, players, on the testimony of the poet and satirist Anthony Nixon, are still "as famous in pride and idlenes, as they are dissolute in living."[33] William Vaughan reports that Gentlemen of the Inns of Court are still squandering their time at plays.[34] And women also, as the poet Richard Brathwait alleges. This writer can recall "a Gentlewoman of our owne Nation, who so daily bestowed the expence of her best houres upon the Stage, as being surprized by sicknesse, even unto death, she became so deafe to such as admonished her of her end, as shee clozed her dying scene with a vehement calling on Hieronimo."[35]

Brathwait is scrupulous in allowing some merit to the theatre. Although he insists that "Time is too precious to be made a Pageant or Morrice on,"[36] he is willing to concede that as playgoers "shall see much lightnesse, so they may heare something worthy more serious attention."[37] Potentially, he thinks, the "judicious hearer" may gather "many excellent precepts for instruc-

[32] Northbrooke, K3.

[33] *The Blacke-yeare*, 1606, C3. See also, for a similar critique, Simon Smel-Knave, *Fearefull and Lamentable Effects of two dangerous Comets*, ?1590, p. 11.

[34] *The Golden Grove*, 1608, Bk. iv, Ch. xxxiv.

[35] *English Gentlewoman*, pp. 53f.

[36] P. 92. [37] *English Gentleman*, 1633, p. 183.

tion, sundry fearefull examples for caution, divers notable occurrents or passages" which he can apply to "no small profit." His time is "not altogether fruitlessly spent." It is faint praise, and overset in what follows. Consideration requires of the purposive man that he "wholy condemne the daily frequenting of" the theatre by gentlemen "who, for want of better imployment, make it their Vocation," abandoning themselves to a compound of "idle words": to "things frivolous, fables, old-wives tales."[38] The scintilla of profit is not so considerable as to compensate for the waste of time involved in "saluting . . . the Afternoone with a Play or a Pallet repose."[39] Neither can it extenuate the "prodigall, sinfull, vaine expence of money."[40] That is Prynne in *Histriomastix*, the Leviathan of all the diatribes written against the stage.

The Puritan casuist addresses himself to "the charges that are laid out upon one stage play," or to the "great cost [that] is vainely, and with hurt bestowed" in the theatre,[41] not as his taste is sour but as it is cultivated. He is not commending a Spartan existence. On the contrary: he understands how to ameliorate that existence. This understanding informs Gosson's indictment of the "infinite Poets, and Pipers, and suche peevishe cattel among us in Englande, that live by merry begging, mainteined by almes, and privily encroch upon every mans purse."[42] After all, the Puritan has not received his deserts. It is not true that he abominates beauty.

[38] *Gentleman*, pp. 185, 194, 195, 186.
[39] *Gentlewoman*, p. 29. [40] P. 310.
[41] Ames, *Cases of Conscience*, p. 217.
[42] *School of Abuse*, B1.

Only he believes (with Thomas Carlyle) that "the un-redeemed ugliness is that of a slothful People." The summons is not to asceticism, as in the fulminations of Gregory the Great, but to aggrandizement. It is to the building of the kingdom of God upon earth. To come to the kernel is hopefully to prosecute this grand de-sign. "What is there left of delight in the world?" Pope Gregory, who is the type of the earlier Puritan, utters his mournful question in a time of the breaking of na-tions. The Lombard is at the gates. The latterday Puri-tan is more buoyant, as he thinks that the future be-longs to him.

> Show me a People energetically busy; heaving, struggling, all shoulders at the wheel; their heart pulsing, every muscle swelling, with man's energy and will;—I show you a People of whom great good is already predicable; to whom all manner of good is yet certain, if their energy endure (*Past and Present*).[43]

The furious pity of Catholic France which Colbert, the great minister of Louis XIV, evinces, turns on his desire to realize this good in the present. Colbert (who endeavors to raise the age at which priests may be or-dained) sins in envy of Protestant Holland as that more prudent nation has rid itself of the army of malingering clerics. This same abhorrence of waste and the dissipat-ing of energy is the key to the praxis of Francis Bacon, about whom his panegyrist Macaulay is more nearly right than is generally supposed. Bacon abandons his studies at Trinity College, Cambridge, not as he is in-different to learning but as he is insistent that learning

[43] Bk. iii, Ch. xii.

avail. It is for this reason that he deprecates masques and triumphs.[44] As a young man who has not yet witnessed the Pisgah-sight, he is willing to take part in the Senecan drama of Gray's Inn; but not as he grows older and more sanguine. William Prynne arraigns the theatre precisely as he is sanguine. Observe that what Prynne is contending against is not simply the expending of money and time but the "mispence of much precious time," and the "mispence of money,"[45] which ought on his view to be diverted to more progressive uses.

Progress is realized in the preferring of the ant to the impecunious grasshopper, who fiddles away the time (Geoffrey Whitney);[46] or in the approving of a new species of more intense and narrow man (to which Pius V testifies obliquely when, in his Bull of Excommunication against the Queen, he complains that she has filled the royal council with "obscure men who are heretics"); or in the proliferating of masters and wardens in the London Livery Companies, whose fathers might have dug for alum in Yorkshire, or worked as salters in Northumberland or Durham, or as tributers in the tin mines of Cornwall. The progress of the clergyman falters, however, as the people intermit their attendance on "Godly lectures" and "flock thick and threefould to the Playhouses," leaving "the Temple of God ... bare and empty."[47]

It is not unnatural that the clergyman should be incensed, like the Reverend William Crashaw, at a preferring of "the immediate devise of the Divell," which is the theatre, "before the holy and immediate ordinance

---

[44] Essay xxxvii.
[45] *Histriomastix*, pp. 305-307, 39.
[46] *Emblemes*, V4.
[47] I. G., *Refutation*, H3v.

of God."[48] This preference is remarked, toward the end of the sixteenth century, by an anonymous moralist who laments that "the playhouses are pestered when the churches are naked. At the one it is not possible to get a place, at the other void seats are plenty."[49] Thomas Lupton, who is describing the laws and customs of the model community of Mauqsun (Nusquam or nowhere), observes ruefully that the people, "immediately after the preching is ended, do come flocking and thronging one another, to the preacher, to whom (being a man of such godliness, conscience and credite) they most willingly, freely, and liberally do deliver mony." That is how it is in Mauqsun. In England, those "that goe hastily, and willingly, and throng one another, striving who shall pay first," are on their way "to see Bear baitings, Bull baitings, Playes, Vauters [fortune tellers], and Tumblers." Siuqila (Aliquis or anyone), who reports them, knows whereof he speaks. He has come lately from Ailgna (England), where the people "are such as seldom heares sermons."[50] In that country, "more have recourse to Playing houses, then to Praying houses."[51] A friend of the theatre expresses mock indignation. "If these be the fruits of playing," says Dick Tarleton, " 'tis time the practisers were expeld."[52]

The preacher, who feels acutely the decline of his own popularity, disparages the theatre very candidly as it draws the people from the temple of God. Or else

[48] *Parable of Poison*, p. 24.

[49] Quoted in E. H. Miller, *Professional Writer in Elizabethan England*, p. 72. Rainolds also attacks the stage as drawing people from sermons (Young, *Transactions*, p. 629).

[50] *Siuqila*, pp. 26f.   [51] *This Worlds Folly*, Blv.

[52] *Kind-Harts Dreame*, E2v.

65

he wishes that playing be forbidden at least on the Sabbath.[53] His agitation is shared by "the Vinters, Alewives, and Victuallers" who, according to Thomas Nashe, "surmise, if there were no Playes, they should have all the company that resort to them, lie bowzing and beerebathing in their houses every after-noone."[54] Not only the churches and taverns but "the Bouling-allyes in Bedlam . . . [are] wont in the after-noones to be left empty, by the recourse of good fellows unto the unprofitable recreation of Stage-playing." The dicing houses have reason "to make sute againe for . . . [the] longer restraint [of plays], though the sicknesse cease." Even the whores are incensed that the "Players should hinder their takings a peny."[55]

The supposed mendacity of the theatre—its penchant for representing fabulous or immoral stories—is not much at issue here. The clerical follower of Wyclif, who denounces the theatre in a late fourteenth-century sermon, has an eye to more intimate matters in suggesting that his parishioners forbear to spend their money in attendance at plays and divert it to him, as by paying "ther rente and ther dette."[56] That is the position which the Reverend John Northbrooke is advocating when, in a dialog between Youth and Age, he advises the young

---

[53] John Walsal, *A Sermon Preached at Pauls Crosse*, 5 Oct. 1578, E5v; John Stockwood, *A Sermon Preached at Paules Crosse on Barthelmew day*, 24 Aug. 1578—repeated 10 May 1579. Stockwood, the headmaster of Tonbridge school, has, in his attack on the theatre, the powerful backing of the Sidneys. R. Howell, *Sir Philip Sidney*, p. 172, describes him as protected by Sir Henry, the poet's father; *DNB* assigns this protection to Sir Robert, the poet's brother.

[54] *Pierce Penilesse*, 1592, F4.   [55] *Kind-Harts Dreame*, E2v-3.
[56] Thompson, *Controversy*, p. 33.

man (it might be Bacon at Gray's Inn) not to patronize
the theatre but the church. Lord Leicester is a patron
of the theatre, as also of the dissenting clergyman John
Field, who rejoices in the collapse of Paris Garden and
—sequentially, I think—runs foul of the law by at-
tacking the authority of the bishops. Episcopacy, and
blood sports (like the baiting of bears and bulls), and
also the maunderings of poets and playwrights, are part
of a single congeries to the man outside the pale. When
Field is released from prison, on Leicester's intercession
(1581), he is prompt to instruct his master, whose
largesse has "nourished . . . impure enterludes and
playes," in the impropriety of serving God and Mam-
mon.[57] The perspicacity of Falstaff is attested, as he sees
how to appropriate to the King's tavern the money
that is earmarked for the King's exchequer.

It is distasteful to the businessman that "whiles
Playes are usde, halfe the day is by most youthes that
hath liberty spent uppon them, or at least the greatest
company drawne to the places where they frequent."
The businessman pays "great rentes"; and so he thinks
it "greate shame, that the houses of retailers neare the
Townes end, should be . . . impoverished" by the con-
tinuing of plays. His conclusion is unimpeachable: "If
they were supprest, the flocke of yoong people would be
equally parted."[58] These plays are more seductive (they
offer more vigorous competition) in that they cost com-
paratively little. When put against the hue and cry
after waste, this seems an inconsequent objection. It is,
however, true, and a sobering fact for the businessman

[57] E. Rosenberg, *Leicester*, pp. 254f.
[58] *Kind-Harts Dreame*, E2v-3.

to ponder, that admission to the public theatres is not so dear as fuel or clothing, or a quart of ale or a pipe of tobacco, or dinner abroad or a ride on the Thames.[59] As these disagreeable comparisons are borne home to the London Corporation which does the bidding of business, the theatre is stigmatized as immoral. It is an acceptable euphemism.

Jeremy Collier, in his attack on the theatre, is stimulated by moral indignation, as also by "an Alderman of London . . . [who] sent him 20 guineas."[60] In Farquhar's comedy the *Constant Couple* (1700), Alderman Smuggler, who cannot see "what business has a prentice at a playhouse," pays a complaisant scribbler 5 guineas to write a tirade against the stage (v, ii). This tirade is anticipated in the lurid disclosures of William Rankins, a needy playwright and poet who panders to the virulent taste of the City,[61] and afterwards writes plays for Nottingham's Men at the Rose. The Theatre and Curtain are places of immoral resort: Rankins, holding up his concave glass, sees them collectively as the Chapel Adulterinum. But that is a disingenuous critique. Mostly, the opponent of the theatres is not so covert. His essential bias is communicated in the story of a thrifty man "dwelling in Holbourne." Although this man is possessed of "great wealth and [is] therfore the meeter

[59] E. Hubler, *The Sense of Shakespeare's Sonnets*, p. 116; Harbage, *Shakespeare's Audience*, p. 59.

[60] The charge that Collier's *Short View* is subsidized is John Oldmixon's, in his *History of England*, quoted in Sister R. Anthony, *Collier Stage Controversy*, p. 8. An anonymous rejoinder to Collier's critique dwells on his supposed pecuniary motive (Anthony, p. 22).

[61] *A Mirror of Monsters*, 1587. Thompson, p. 89, conjectures that Rankins was bribed.

for company," "yet if any freend or neighbour require him to goe with them to the Tavern, to the Ale house, to the Theater, to the Curtain . . . or to Paris garden or any such place of expence: he utterly refuseth." But this refusal of his is not churlish, as the sequel attests:

> After their return that willed his company, his maner is to go unto some one of them, desiring him to tel him truely what hee hath spent since his going foorth, which having learned at him whether it be a grote or sixpence, more or lesse, hee goeth straight unto a Cofer that hee hath standing secretly in his Chamber, which hath a Til . . . [in] which he putteth in asmuch mony as the party said that [he] had spent, and this til he never openeth untill the end of the yeer, so often times hee findeth ther in forty shillings, oft times three or foure pound or more.[62]

Shakespeare's character is very foolish, who "had rather than forty shillings" his "book of Songs and Sonnets here."

Actors are "brawlers, roisters, lovers, loiterers, ruffians"; the theatres in which they play are "brothel houses of Bawdery." This conclusion is asserted by the renegade playwright Anthony Munday. The relation between the effect and the cause is not altogether mysterious: Munday's *Second and third blast of retrait from plaies and theatres* (1580) features on its title page the emblazoned arms of the Corporation of London.[63] In Jonson's comedy, the pastor of Amsterdam must rail against plays as he would please the alderman whose daily custard he devours (*Alchemist*, III, ii). It is

[62] T. F., *Newes from the North,* 1579, I.iv.
[63] C. T. Wright, *Anthony Munday,* Ch. v; Ringler, *Gosson,* pp. 26-28.

this alderman who appoints the sermons delivered at Paul's Cross in denunciation of the theatre, as by William Crashaw, or by the Oxford divine Robert Bolton, whose *Generall Directions for a Comfortable Walking with God* are founded on the proposition that the theatre is inimical to the husbanding of money and time.[64] Crashaw condemns the players as there is no profit in them: "they have no calling, but are in the State like warts on the hand, or blemishes in the face." The magistrate, like zealous Phinehas, the high priest of the Jews, is exhorted to take "just vengeance on that publike dishonour" with which the commonweal is plagued.[65] This plague is notably infectious. The colonizing of the New World is understood to be menaced by the players: Crashaw in a sermon to the planters of Virginia (1610). They are "enemies to this Plantation . . . because we resolve to suffer no Idle persons in Virginia, which course if it were taken in England, they know they . . . [must] turn to new occupations."

The idle trade with which they occupy the present is "but as crackling of thornes under a pot." Bolton, who ventures the analogy, desires the putting down of stage plays and kindred recreations as they are "costly"—it is his first consideration—and as they are "ingrossers of time" for which "We must bee countable" at the "great and generall Audit." At this audit, a bill of particulars will be required "for every farthing; how thou gotst it; with what warrant thou kepst it; upon what thou

---

[64] Bolton anticipates this attack on the stage in *A Discourse of True Happiness*, 1612, delivered at Oxford and St. Paul's.
[65] Sermon of Feb. 14, 1607, pp. 171f.

70

spentst it."[66] It will not suffice to plead the laying out of money on "prophane and obscene Playes." The theatre enfeebles "all manly resolution," or it sustains the "noisome wormes that cankar and blast the generous and noble buds" of the kingdom. As men delight in these "abominable spectacles," their will to be up and doing "melteth as the winter ice, and floweth away as unprofitable waters." The requiting of the playgoer is not reserved, however, to the Last Day.

Here poetry and politics manifest their intimate connection. As the patron of stage plays makes nothing "for the publike good," God will root him out of the land "as a fruitlesse and faithlesse nation . . . and let out his vineyard to other husbandmen, which will deliver Him the fruites in their seasons."[67] John Rainolds, who is looking for an epigraph to introduce his meditations on Church and Scripture, finds the appropriate text in Jeremiah: "We would have healed Babylon, but she is not healed: forsake her, O ye children of God, and let us go every one into his own country" (51:9). This better country is the Commonwealth of Oliver Cromwell.

Already the short way of the Protector is suggested, in the attempt of "the pious Magistrates" of London to achieve "the suppressing of common houses for Enterludes, and Dicing, and Carding." The *Monster Late Found Out* and published to the world by the mechanic preacher Richard Rawlidge honors these magistrates as they urge the Privy Council to take order with plays and

[66] *General Directions*, pp. 169, 154f., 157, 165f.
[67] *Discourse of True Happiness*, N1, C3v.

71

to "thrust those Players out of the Citty." It is a case in which the right hand knows what the left hand is doing. The "many great and crying sinnes" hatched in the playhouse boil down to this: that players "undoe and begger many hundreds" as they are efficient in filching money from the pockets of "the industrious and honest Citizen."[68] What is chiefly obnoxious in "those mercenary Squitter-wits mis-called Poets" is that their "pickepocket Inventions can *Emungere plebes argento*, slily nip the bunges of the baser troopes."[69] The voice is the voice of Ancient Pistol; the hand is that of the London Corporation.

In the later seventeenth century, an annalist of the old immoral age before the doors of the theatres were closed to the baser troops remembers that "the Judges, the Templars [lawyers], and the Puritans of all professions and conditions, being very sensible how the youth was alienated from religion and corrupted by cards, dice, revels, plays, and interludes . . . engaged [many Puritans] to write against them."[70] In this company, Stephen Gosson is specifically included. His preferment follows. The *School of Abuse*, which is the instrument of Gosson's new fortunes, enjoys a first printing of 3,000 copies, as against the normal run of 500. It is not religious fervor—or not entirely—that inspires the publishers to undertake this extraordinary issue. Presumably the proceeds are already in hand before a single copy is sold. At first, and as he is blind to the light, Gosson becomes a poor player and a maker of plays. Subsequently, having hearkened to "godly preachers . . . at Paules crosse,"

[68] 1628, pp. 2-4, 29.   [69] *This Worlds Folly*, B3.
[70] Roger Morrice, MS I, fol. 615 (6); in Ringler's *Gosson*, p. 28.

72

as also to their more pragmatic sponsors, he discovers a great antipathy to "the abhominable practises of playes." The apologist for the theatre ("the strawe where the padd lurks") is stigmatized as a purveyor of "guttes and garbage." The playwright, who dramatizes the wanton exploits of mythological persons, is more noisome. Here Gosson is reminiscent of the early Christian poet Prudentius, and not least in his enthusiastic reception of the classical past. "Apollo was a buggerer, and Schoolemaister of perjurie; Mars a murderer, Mercury a theefe, Castor & Pollux, whome they reporte to be twinnes growen in one body, when they were ravishers of other mens wives, never mette within one payre of sheets." The regenerate playwright resolves to "dwell in earth, for heaven is full of whores." As he publicizes this resolution, his way is smoothed by employment as a tutor in the country, and perhaps as a government agent. At last he is rewarded with a series of ecclesiastical appointments. He ends his days as the incumbent of one of the richest livings in London.

In a letter to the Lord Mayor "and the right worshipful his brethren," Gosson suggests tactfully that "when they are beste advised" they will "banishe their Players."[71] But that is to preach to the converted. Sir Richard Pipe, whose attention is solicited, bears a part in framing the Licensing Order (December 6, 1574) which decrees approval of plays by the Mayor and Aldermen.[72] This approval is very temperate. The poet and romancer Thomas Lodge, essaying an ill-considered "defence of playes and play makers" that falls in by and large with

---

[71] *School of Abuse*, B2-v, L3-4v, E8v.
[72] Ringler, pp. 26f., 27f., 49.

Gosson's animadversions, is denied a license to publish by "the godly and reverent that had to deale in the cause."[73]

That is inequitable treatment but it is not surprising. The godly and reverent make a fetish of putting shoulders to the wheel. It is for this reason that the Elizabethan Poor Law, invoking punishment on "ruffians, Vagabondes and Masterles men," lumps together, "among roges and idle persons"—I am quoting from William Harrison's *Description of Britain* (1577)— "Cosiners . . . practizers of Phisiognomy and Palmestry, tellers of fortunes, fencers, bearwards . . . minstrels, jugglers, pedlers, tinkers"—and "players." But that these players are masterless is only a convenient stick with which to beat them. The attack does not abate when, by the end of the century, they have acquired redoubtable patrons. The town of Leicester complains of players, not because they are vagabonds but because it lacks or grudges the wherewithal to pay them (1566). By authority of the Master of Revels or the noble patron in whose service the players are enrolled, traveling companies are made free of "town halls, moot halls, guild halls, schoolhouses," as they journey in the provinces. Local officialdom, if this freedom is not to its taste, has no recourse but to emulate the church-wardens of the village of Syston, who must hand over a gratuity "to Lord Morden's players because they should not play in the church" (1602).

In the year in which Shakespeare's First Folio is

[73] Dedication to the Gentlemen of the Inns of Court, *Alarum against Usurers*, 1584, p. 37; reprinted in Lodge's *Defense of Poetry*, 1853.

74

published, the city of Norwich decides to follow a less placatory course. The Privy Council is requested to bar access to players of interludes. What inspires the agitation of the city is the loss or diverting of the working-man's wages.[74] The money he makes burns a hole in his pocket; the theatre, like adamant, draws this money to itself. When the Court of Aldermen addresses a remonstrance against the players to the Archbishop of Canterbury (1592), the arguments it cites are not pietistic but social. The important charge, reiterated at London in the closing years of Elizabeth's reign, is that they entice "apprentices and other servants from their ordinary workes."[75] The businessman's anguish, than which none is more piercing, throbs in the indictment of strolling players at Coventry (1615), who are felt as meriting censure exactly as they excel in "drawing of the artificers and common people from their labour."[76] A half century later, at Norwich, a city which apparently went from bad to worse, the businessman is still complaining of the theatre, which is said to "divert the meaner sort" from their employment "in the manufactories, thereby occasioning a vain expense of time and money."[77]

The preacher, in voicing his objection to the stage, is not so candid as the businessman. Perhaps that is to do him less than justice. Perhaps he is more nearly disinterested a critic. He complains of the theatre as the forging house of Satan. Its commitment is to specious

---

[74] 1623; Chambers, *Elizabethan Stage*, I, 387.

[75] July 28, 1597; "Dramatic Records of the City of London: the Remembrancia," *Malone Society Collection*, I, Pt. 1, 80; Harbage, p. 14.

[76] *Elizabethan Stage*, I, 338, n. 3.

[77] S. M. Rosenfeld, *Strolling Players*, p. 36.

representation, whence slothfulness and lack of purpose derive. The critique from the side of morality tends, however, to merge, in its issue and purport, with crasser considerations of mine and thine. "Show me a liar," says the proverb, "and I will show thee a thief."[78] The mendacity in which the theatre is understood to traffic involves, necessarily, the expense of money and time.

[78] George Herbert, *Jacula Prudentum.*

IV

The Day of Darkness and the Gospel of Gain

IT IS TO stanch this expense that the effort is made, with the assiduous support of the clergy, to compel the masters and wardens of the London Livery Companies to forbid plays to their apprentices, servants, and journeymen.[1] The meaner sort—like Ralph the prentice in the *Knight of the Burning Pestle*—as their bent is to pictures and things, prove, however, intractable. They do not concur in the judgment of Oliver Cromwell, who supposes austerely that "the mind is the man."[2] That is an unreasonable supposition and curiously definitive of the great panegyrists of human reason: like Plato, whose impatience with semblables is vindicated at last in the closing of all theatres by edict (1642), as the Rule of the Saints is accomplished.

This Rule, like the ideal state which Plato imagines in the *Laws*, or Sir Thomas More in *Utopia*, is hopeful; it is even heroic. But like the Platonic state, it opposes the spirit to the letter, and so assures its own destruction and the perverting of the spirit itself. More, describing his communistic society, appears to affirm this opposition, as also in the contempt he shares with his adversary Tyndale for the superficial character of medieval romance.

---

[1] Harbage, *Shakespeare's Audience*, p. 69, quotes "Dramatic Records of the City of London," in *Malone Society Collection*, II, Pt. III, p. 313.

[2] John Buchan, *Oliver Cromwell*, p. 464.

But More is concurrently, in his allegiance to ceremonious (or superficial) observances, among the last great representatives, on the public stage, of the old-fashioned psychology or temper.

The deprecating of ceremony—whatever is of the surface—is a natural consequence of the exalting of mind over matter. The issue, paradoxically, is the triumph of mindlessness, and at last the ascendancy of a grossly materialistic point of view. An anecdote of the Commonwealth period illustrates how this unexpected result is accomplished, as the body and the spirit, or the letter and the spirit, are divorced. To the parishioners of a village church in Surrey, a Parliamentary soldier appears, bearing five candles in token of the five lights or salient points of his vision. As these points are enumerated, the candles are extinguished, one by one. First, the abolition of the Sabbath is commanded; next, the abolition of tithes. Each is "merely ceremonial," and the second "a discouragement of industry and tillage." (Compare the critique of the theatre as mendacious and, consequently, as wasteful of money and time.) Ministers also are rejected as useless, "now Christ himself descends into the hearts of his Saints." Magistrates are put away, as they tie themselves "to laws and ordinances, mere human inventions." Even the Word of God, encapsulated in the Bible, is tainted or it is nugatory. The Bible offers "beggarly rudiments, milk for Babes. But now Christ is in glory amongst us, and imparts a fuller measure of his Spirit to his Saints, than this [book] can afford." And so the soldier applies his final candle to the leaves of Holy Writ.[3]

[3] From *Anarchia Anglicana*, 1649, quoted in A. Simpson, *Puritanism in Old and New England*, pp. 54f.

The canons and responsibilities are disputed, on which life in society depends. Utopia, as the Antinomian conceives it, is the reign of anarchy and naked self-interest. See, as a gloss on the interdicting of laws and letters, the emancipated commonwealth hypothesized by Gonzalo in the *Tempest*, and the subsequent behavior of the villains in that play. Nature imitates art. The dream of the holy synod on earth is enacted not in the building of Jerusalem but in the making of that new England whose coming is announced in the elevation of Thomas Cromwell and dramatized in the beheading of Thomas More, whose dedication is conveyed in the words which the Renaissance merchant prince Datini causes to be inscribed on the first page of his ledgers: "In the name of God and of profit," whose tendency is realized in Plugson of Undershot, whose apotheosis is the Coketown of *Hard Times*.

This England the splenitive Shakespeare divines and excoriates in *Timon of Athens*; or he eschews it altogether, as in the fourth act of the *Winter's Tale*, for an elegant hameau of his own devising, hooked out of time and place. In the allegory of the *Tempest*, he offers in its room a rival creation; in *As You Like It*, he composes a bucolic lament for an age already and irremediably past. *Et in Arcadia ego*: even in the golden world of pastoral, from which the fabulous Duke and his courtiers have banished the peremptory summons of time, the end of this tranquil order is preparing. "O good old man," says Shakespeare's hero Orlando to Adam, the faithful retainer:

> how well in thee appears
> The constant service of the antique world,
> When service sweat for duty, not for meed!

79

It is, however, not the servant but the sentimental master who prunes a rotten tree: that is how a modern Adam might retort on another Orlando.

The self-effacing retainer is applauded as he defers to an ideal remote from material satisfaction. It is this ideal to which the artist pays allegiance. Nicholas Hilliard (1537-1619), the Elizabethan miniature painter, thinks that no man "could have the patience or the leasure to perform any exact true & rare peece of worke" unless indifferent "to those comon cares of the world for food and garment." The artist puts away "emulation and desier . . . [and], not respecting the profitt or the length of time," undertakes to do his "utermost best."[4] In this impersonal dedication, he is profoundly antipathetic to the "fashion of these times,"

> Where none will sweat but for promotion,
> And having that do choke their service up.

The new and more tenacious hostility to art is sequential. "Poetry, in this latter age," as Ben Jonson discovers to his cost, "hath proved but a mean mistress, to such as have wholly addicted themselves to her." The negligent saying of the poet that punctuality is the thief of time is a noxious saying to the man of business. "There is scarce one shire in Wales or England, where . . . [his] moneys are not Lent out at Usury": Philip Massinger in the *City Madam* (1632). It follows—as to the London Merchant in Lillo's tragedy *manqué*, supposed to take place in the year of the Armada—that "we must not let artificers lose their time, so useful to the public and their families, in unnecessary attendance" (1, i). This mer-

---

[4] *The Arte of Limning*, 1624, p. 15.

chant is homiletic by temperament. He is also a practical man. The language he uses is, suggestively, the same language as that employed by the opponents of the theatre. The moralist Primaudaye is very much of his party in supposing it "a shameful thing . . . to lose time that ought to be so precious unto us," but not in unnecessary attendance, rather "in beholding and in hearing players."[5] In the strictures of the moralist as of the entrepreneur, the same bias governs. Each bears out the truth of Montaigne's irreverent observation: "Between ourselves, two things have always seemed to me in singular accord, supercelestial opinions and subterranean morals."[6]

The Renaissance is many-sided, like its most celebrated playwright. I suppose the near relation of money and time to have been lost on the urban proletariat, whose standard of living declined sharply toward the end of Elizabeth's reign. In this period, philanthropy undergoes a tremendous expansion—but in lagging relation to need.[7] In the earlier seventeenth century Sir Arthur Ingram, the greatly successful and meanly rapacious financier, endows a hospital for poor widows at Bootham. Anticipating praise for his pious behavior, Ingram courts an opinion of the almshouse. A gentleman from Leeds, as the anecdote reports him, complains of the size of the building. Sir Arthur is perplexed. "Why," he expostulates, "the rooms are big enough and it is every man's choice what numbers he will admit." Nevertheless, says the candid respondent, the

[5] *The French Academy*, trans. 1586.
[6] *Essays*, iii, xiii.
[7] W. K. Jordan, *Philanthropy in England*.

81

building "is too little to hold those that you have undone."[8]

The course of this undoing is reflected in the swelling coffers of the landed gentleman or entrepreneur.[9] The afflux of precious metals from the new world, as it flows through a narrow bore, widens the gap between the many and the few. In towns like Lincoln, houses fall empty; Bristol and Coventry, in the middle years of the century, are economically stagnant.[10] So far, perhaps, the difference between past and present is not especially remarkable. In other and less propitious times, men pursue their advantage. Trade goes forward. The middle class fulfills its customary function: it rises. And yet the Renaissance is ascertainably peculiar. Exceptions prove the rule.

In the more constricted England of Richard II, a cleric like William of Wykeham transcends his modest background to become the royal chancellor and the founder of New College, Oxford. "Manners makyth man": that is William's motto, and apparently it is verified in the event. But this event is touched with magic: that is why it is memorable. In the England of Elizabeth, aggression is more consistently rewarded. The difference is not one of degree but of kind.

The old-fashioned man is blind to the difference, and so he misses the more literal construction of the Biblical

---

[8] A. F. Upton, *Sir Arthur Ingram*, p. 263.

[9] R. H. Tawney, *The Agrarian Problem*, describes the flow of money and land throughout the sixteenth century from the peasantry to the great proprietors. See esp. Tawney's moving summation, pp. 404-409.

[10] Ramsey, *Tudor Economic Problems*, pp. 113, 102.

saying, which is also an injunction: "Wherefore do ye spend money for that which is not bread? and your labor for that which satisfieth not?" (Isaiah 55:2) In this way it happens that his place is preempted by a more pragmatic kind of man, who understands—in the cold phrase of an *arriviste* like the Lord Treasurer Burghley—that "a man can buy nothing in the market with gentility."[11] Sir Philip Sidney, who thinks mistakenly that his "cheefest honor is to be a Dudley," fails of this hardheaded understanding.[12] For that reason he is put to ask, in his celebrated *Apologie for Poetrie*, "why England (the Mother of excellent mindes) should bee growne so hard a step-mother to Poets." The poet deplores the new relation; but he is constrained to accept it.

It is Pride by which the angels fell. Sidney, who is defending his uncle the Earl of Leicester, is very tiresome in supposing "that he who was by right of blood . . . the awncientest Viscount of England, heir in blood and Armes to the first or second Earl of England, in blood of inheritance a Gray, a Talbot, a Beauchamp" andsoforth, must take precedence over all the world besides.[13] But already, in the waning Middle Ages, the sin of Pride is displaced by a more powerful and more seductive temptation. Mankind, who is proof against the solicitings of the World, the Flesh, and the Devil, succumbs at last to Covetousness, in the fifteenth-century morality play, the *Castle of Perseverance*. Now the im-

---

[11] Letters to his son Robert Cecil, on the importance of marrying well; Bowen, *Lion and the Throne*, p. 117.

[12] Pp. 65f. in *Defence of the Earl of Leicester*: Feuillerat ed., Vol. III.

[13] *Defence*, p. 67.

pulse to gain ranks first in the hierarchy of sins, as the pursuit of gain is so richly rewarded.

The improvident aristocrat declines in his pride or incapacity to engage in this pursuit. "The practise of mechanicall and vile trade is proper to him ignoble": Count Annibale Romei.[14] "He detesteth all gainfull wayes," says the historian Thomas Fuller, and scorns the scarlet robes of the merchant as having "a stain of the stamell die in them."[15] His scorn begets the loss of his encumbered estates.[16] "How could merchants thrive," the playwright John Marston inquires, "if gentlemen were not unthrift?" (*Eastward Ho!* 1605) The Crown attempts to stand against the erosion of its landed supporters, as by circumscribing in law the rapacity and privilege of the mortgagee.[17] But the effort to stop the

[14] *The Courtier's Academie*, trans. 1598, p. 199.

[15] *The Holy State*, 1642, Bk. IV, Ch. xii.

[16] L. Stone, in *The Crisis of the Aristocracy*, and in his "Anatomy of the Elizabethan Aristocracy," *EHR* (1948), pp. 1-53, documents the "attrition of the economic resources" of the "ancient descended" gentleman (p. 37). A. Simpson, *Wealth of the Gentry*, argues for relative stability: "continuity, rather than change, is the keynote. . . . The agrarian history of this century has turned out to be far more prosaic than . . . expected" (p. 216). H. R. Trevor-Roper, "Anatomy Anatomized," *EHR* (1951), 279-98, attacks Stone's figures as inaccurate and misleading. Tawney on the decline of the aristocracy and the rise of the gentry is also assailed as suspect (pp. 294f.). But see Tawney's persuasive defense in "Postscript," *EHR* (1954), 91-97.

[17] Statute 2HVIII c.8 forbids the mortgagee to take any part of the revenue yielded by an estate on which he had advanced money. In Elizabeth's first Parliament, Cecil proposes a limitation of 50 pounds a year on land which merchants (London aldermen or sheriffs excepted) might acquire. Thomas Wilson, *A Discourse upon Usury*, 1572; ed. Tawney, 1925, p. 41. And see Stone, "Elizabethan Aris-

drift is unavailing. Early in the reign of Charles I, it is reported of the House of Commons that its members are "able to buy the upper house (his majesty only excepted) thrice over."[18] This spectacular competence is not achieved by cultivating the Muses. "He dissuaded me from Poetry," says Drummond of Ben Jonson, "for that she had beggered him, when he might have been a rich lawyer, Physitian or Marchant."

The new and more acquisitive protagonist, as personated by Sir Giles Overreach in Philip Massinger's dramatic tract for the England of the early Stuarts, *A New Way to Pay Old Debts*, or by Sir Luke Frugal in Massinger's *City Madam*, does not need to be dissuaded from poetry. Neither is he much preoccupied with the higher learning. As Massinger begins his *City Madam*, Sir John Frugal has just made "payment on the nail for a Manor." It is the more fruitful mode of proceeding that denotes him. "Stand not on forme," Overreach advises, "Words are no substances." Like the Puritan divine, he deplores the wasting of time on "wanton Pictures and spectacles," and commends instead an intimate acquaintance "with the gaine of godlinesse"—or else with the godliness of gain. Those who prosecute this more rewarding acquaintance "are like provident and thrifty Merchants, who being set upon their profit, suffer not their mindes to range after pleasures, but busily follow their trade which bringeth in commodity."[19]

tocracy," for the "crucial role played by the Crown in support of aristocratic revenues" (p. 32).

[18] *The Court and Times of Charles the First*, ed. R. F. Williams, 1848, I, 331.

[19] Rogers, *Practice of Christianitie*, 1623, Bk. II, cap, 6, p. 137; cap. 14, p. 206.

The opposition is that between the leaf and the indolent flower. In the sixteenth century, it is by resort to some such metaphor as this that kinds and classes of men are recognized and evaluated. Now the mendicant, who used to be a hallowed figure, begins to be despised. "To be a Christian is no idle trade."[20] Beggars, as they dispute the proposition, are "lewd, lazy drones, unprofitable burdens of the earth, and intolerable caterpillers of the Common wealth." In this latter day, "they are . . . to be compelled to worke for their maintenance."[21] Inutility describes the "idle monks and wanton canons" —Ascham's phrase—with whom the Reformation takes order.

> We are poor bedemen of Your Grace
> We pray for your deceased ancestrees
> For whom we sing masses and dirigees [dirges]
> And succor their souls in needful haste.

That is how the monks respond (on the word of a satirical pamphleteer) to the accusation that they fail to give succor to the prince (in this case, to Henry VIII). The poet and playwright John Lyly, to whom the dissolution of the monasteries is ancient history, can scarcely credit a time when grown men employed themselves in fingering their rosary beads and "ate till they sweat and lay in bed till their bones ached."[22] But this contempt which the poet indulges is dangerous in that it makes against his own condition. "Ease [is] the nurse of poetry," says an aristocratic character in Sidney's novel *Arcadia*. Ease is, however, reprehensible now. The rhetorician George

<hr>

[20] Rogers, *Christianitie*, 1618 ed., p. 505.
[21] Bolton, *Directions*, p. 151.   [22] Hunter's *Lyly*, p. 351.

Puttenham, in his essay in the *Arte of English Poesie* (1589), remarks on the contrast between that "reputation [which] Poesy and Poets . . . [enjoyed] in old time with Princes" and "the scorne and ordinary disgrace offered unto Poets [in] these dayes."[23] Henry Peacham is aware that poets are no longer of "such esteeme, as they have beene in former times"; and Francis Meres, of the diminished respect accorded the poet and playwright, in lamenting the "lacke of Patrones" which characterizes the "ingrateful and damned age."[24]

The age is not ungrateful but sagacious. The kind of activity it is inclined to applaud is fruitful in tangible ways. Poetry, in contrast, is not so fruitful. For that reason, applause is no longer forthcoming. Pragmatic considerations are decisive. The anti-historical or sentimental man opposes to the exacting character of the modern world a roseate past that has no existence, unless in the paintings of Burne-Jones or the nostalgic essays of Ralph Adams Cram.[25] His economic history is personal pleading, and attests to a desire to be angry or hurt. Caesar von Heisterbach, writing in the thirteenth century, scorns the commercial life for the gray celerity and hardness of heart that attend it. As he ranges himself against the way we live now, he is recognizable as a medieval person. This recognition ought also to en-

[23] Bk. i, Ch. viii.

[24] *The Compleat Gentleman*, 1622, Ch. x; *Palladis Tamia*, in G. G. Smith, ii, 313. The decline of patronage is documented by E. H. Miller, *Professional Writer*, pp. 99-105, 131-36; P. Sheavyn, *Literary Profession in the Elizabethan Age*, pp. 5-7, 20-33; and Robert Clements, "Condemnation of the Poetic Profession," *SP*, XLIII (1946), 220-30.

[25] See, e.g., the little book called *Walled Towns*, 1919.

compass (what the sentimentalist is apt to ignore) the appalling cruelty and superstition and the pathological view of sex with which his remarks are suffused. Heisterbach, the pious Cistercian, is able to quote, without recoiling, the battle cry of the Crusader in the Albigensian wars: "Kill them all; God will look after His own."[26]

It is not necessary to invoke Professor Welsh, the panegyrist of Merry England, in support of the modest but consequential thesis that things are no longer as they were. In England, in the seventeenth century, the proposition is verified: "Red-lined accounts are richer than the songs of Grecian years." The London preacher who observes that "God commandeth all men to labour" is not simply prescriptive in lining out a proper regimen for his constituents to follow. He sees that "a slothfull hand maketh poore, as a diligent hand maketh rich."[27] It is open to the diligent hand to make "what is immethodic [and] waste . . . methodic, regulated, arable; obedient and productive": the "forever-enduring Gospel" of Thomas Carlyle.[28] It is in the Renaissance that this Gospel is adumbrated first, as in the new pedagogy of a humanist like Johann Sturm,[29] or in the distillations of Erasmus, or in the new philosophy according to Bacon, or in the dialectics of Peter Ramus, Sturm's pupil in Paris days.

Partly, these formulations manifest an impersonal desire to collaborate with the Creator in bringing order

[26] Heisterbach is quoting Arnald-Amalric, in Z. Oldenbourg, *Massacre at Montségur*, p. 116.

[27] Hill, *Pathway to Prayer*, H8v.

[28] *Past and Present*, Ch. xii, "Reward."

[29] P. 209 in P. Mesnard, "Pedagogy of Johann Sturm," *Studies in the Renaissance*, xiii (1966).

out of chaos. It is the intention of Erasmus, in composing his *Paraphrases*, "to supply gaps, to soften the abrupt, to arrange the confused, to simplify the involved, to untie the knotty, to throw light on the obscure."[30] But the end envisaged differs, in point of material satisfaction, from that imputed to the sterile pursuit of art. In the playhouse, for example, the actors presume—in the words of a hostile critic—for money received, "to render that which is not moneys worth." To this energetic polemicist, who is responding to Thomas Heywood's defense of the theatre, players are "idle drones" and productive of idleness: "for they can take no paines, they know not how to worke, nor in any lawfull calling to get their living: but to avoid labour and worke, like brave and noble beggers, they stand to take money of every one that comes to see them loiter and play." This more strenuous person discovers that playing is anathema, but not for homiletic reasons. He concludes: "I never saw any thing lesse profitable in the common wealth."[31] They are one and the same man, as the actor Dick Tarleton is made to observe, who "maligne our moderate merriments, and thinke there is no felicity but in excessive possession of wealth."[32] I take the conjunction to be of critical importance.

As money is not so fecund in the age of Alaric and Athaulf, the pursuit of money is not so fierce or unremitting. To the semi-barbarous Christian of the dark centuries between Augustine and Alcuin of York, whose unsettled (enervating) existence is lived in perpetual terror, now of the Lombards and now of Islam, time's

[30] Quoted in Farrar, *History of Interpretation*, p. 320.
[31] I. G., *Refutation*, I1-2, G2.   [32] *Kind-Harts Dreame*, E4v.

progress counts for little and is mostly unremarked. The poor verses of Venantius Fortunatus weigh equally with the mottoes on sundials. *Qui satus ex homine est, et moriturus erit*: the sixth-century poet, as he is in step with the lachrymose temper of his time, is not yet the occasion of scandal or reproach. So far, it is the idle virtues that earn the sun. The population of England, in the years just before Elizabeth ascends the throne, has yet to achieve the level it had reached two centuries earlier, on the eve of the great plague (1348).[33] "Who comes of the seed of man, for him death waits." The melancholy saying of Venantius Fortunatus is still approved in daunting ways.

But now abruptly, in the sixteenth century, the size of London triples. The vend or total market of the Newcastle coalfields, which stands at 33,000 tons in the year of Shakespeare's birth, increases within his lifetime almost eightfold.[34]

> Why seek you fire in some exalted sphere?
> Earth's fruitful bosom will supply you here.

That is the antiquary William Camden, on the glory and the promise of Newcastle in his own time.[35] Camden has heard the death knell of the quiescent past in the water-driven hammers beating day and night in the iron and glass industries of the Weald. In his England, drowsy villages are metamorphosed to industrial towns. Leeds and Manchester become synonymous with the

---

[33] 3.75 million in 1438; c.3.22 million, 200 years later. Ramsey, p. 15.

[34] Ramsey, pp. 109, 92. In 1609, the Newcastle vend had reached 252,000 tons.

[35] *Britannia*, 1586; quoted in Ramsey, p. 179.

manufacture of clothing, and Sheffield and Birmingham emblematic of a new iron age. The peasant, whose business had been altogether with the coercing of a little land to sustain a single family, is supplanted by the well-to-do yeoman, who is more spacious in the possession of dirt.

> Have mind, therfore, theyself to hold
> Within the bounds of thy degree.

But this admonishing of the yeoman, as by the moralist Robert Crowley (1550), is no longer to the purpose.[36]

> The Plowman that in times past was contented in Russet, must now adayes have his doublet of the fashion with wide cuts, his garters of fine silke of Granado to meet his Sis on Sunday: the farmer that was contented in times past with his Russet Frocke & Mockado sleeves, now sels a Cow against Easter to buy him silken geere for his credit.[37]

Mobility is the rule, and its direction is substantially upward.

More than 80% of those who work the land abandon their native villages in the century preceding the Civil War. In the long period which extends from Bosworth Field to the Restoration of the Stuarts, only 14 of 172 mayors of London are Londoners born; and, of wealthy testators classified by a modern historian of philanthropy, less than 10%.[38] For liveried merchants and shopkeepers and retailers, this percentage declines even further.[39]

[36] Quoted in Ramsey, p. 133.

[37] Thomas Lodge in *Wits Miserie*, p. 14.

[38] Jordan, *Philanthropy in England*.

[39] Ramsey, pp. 14, 110. Of 813 merchants, only 75 or 9% were London born; of shopkeepers and retailers, 4%

In Massinger's *City Madam*, a lowly butcher begets a constable of the hundred. This more affluent man enjoys the wider margin which any considerable or sophisticated economic activity requires. Disposing of an agricultural surplus which, transmuted into currency, passes over the counters of merchants in the cities, he builds a manor house, or he marries into the gentry: Lady Frugal is the daughter of "an honest Country farmer, Goodman Humble, by his neighbors ne're call'd master." Or else he finances commercial adventures beyond the sea. As these are successful, the gentle blood of his descendants is assured. A yeoman, says Fuller, is "a Gentleman in Ore, whom the next age may see refined."[40] It is by virtue of these impressive advances that Spenser's friend Gabriel Harvey, having "observed the course of Industry . . . and finally found profitt to be our pleasure, provision our security, labour our honour, warfare our welfare," inquires (rhetorically): "who of reckoning can spare any lewde or vaine time for corrupt pamphlets, or who of judgement will not cry away with these paultringe fidlefaddles?"[41] *Quid dant artes?*

When the Puritan divine Richard Rogers introduces his work on the *Practice of Christianitie*, it occurs to him to present it as a "most rich and gainfull trade," one that produces "ample revenue, farre exceeding that of Croesus."[42] Like Canon Chasuble, he is speaking metaphorically. But the choice of the figure is important. Gain is the integer of value. That is why Thorowgood the London Merchant advises Trueman his clerk to study, not

[40] *Holy State*, Bk. ii, Ch. xviii.
[41] *Pierce's Supererogation*, 1593; quoted G. G. Smith, ii, 262.
[42] "Epistle Dedicatorie."

corrupt and paltering pamphlets, but "the method of merchandize":

> See how it is founded in reason and the nature of things. How it has promoted humanity, as it has opened and yet keeps up an intercourse between nations far remote from one another in situation, customs, and religion; promoting arts, industry, peace and plenty, by mutual benefits diffusing mutual love from pole to pole (III, i).

This intercourse of personal and public satisfaction is agreeable to Sir Walter Ralegh, who does not prosper as he composes verses on the holy land of Walsingham, but as he acquires a monopoly over the wine trade, and in the manufacture of cloth and playing cards, and the mining of Cornish tin. Ralegh is unlucky in his end. In the interim, however, he is able to dispose of a palace in the Strand, estates in the Midland counties, and 40,000 acres in Ireland.[43] "Never in the annals of the modern world has there existed so prolonged and so rich an opportunity for the business man, the speculator and the profiteer": Keynes on the early seventeenth century.[44] The jurist Edward Coke is one of those whom the tide bears on to fortune. Coke, at his death in the reign of Charles I, holds title to more than sixty manor houses in England.[45] That is better than the tun of Ca-

[43] Bowen, *Lion and the Throne*, p. 164; Stone, "Elizabethan Aristocracy," p. 28.

[44] *A Treatise on Money*, II, 159. And see F. J. Fisher, "The Development of London as a Centre of Conspicuous Consumption," *Trans. Royal Hist. Soc.*, xxx (1948), 37-50, and esp. p. 42.

[45] Bowen, pp. 527, 552f. And compare the good fortune of an *arriviste* like Burghley, who "might in twenty-one years succeed in acquiring manors, the bare catalogue of which covers no less than six pages" (Stone, "Elizabethan Aristocracy," p. 28).

nary and the laureate crown that are reserved to Ben Jonson.

Already in the Tudor period, opportunity beckons to men of judgment who make profit their pleasure. Sir John Gresham (d. 1556), commencing life as a mercer and putting by his earnings against a sunny day, puts them out again as a sponsor of the Russia Company. His bread comes back on the waters pure gold. His brother Sir Richard (1485?-1549) supplies a grateful nobility with capital and watches it quicken: in the decade before his death he is able to purchase the abbey of Fountains at a cost of 11,000 pounds. Each of the Greshams becomes Lord Mayor of London. Richard's son Sir Thomas is the founder of the Royal Exchange. The account books of Thomas Gresham for the last years of King Edward VI, as they indicate net profits of nearly 15%, imply a doubling of his capital every five years.[46]

This implication is stimulating, as to the Jacobean businessman Lionel Cranfield, who begins as a London apprentice, marries into the nobility, and rises to the office of receiver of customs. It is the apposite title. In his subsequent capacity as master of the Court of Wards, Cranfield grows familiar with the pockets of litigants and suitors, who are instructed thereby in the value of his time. At last (and just before his imprisonment for peculation) he is Baron Cranfield and Earl of Middlesex. He does not ascend the ladder as he excogitates idle words. Cranfield writes financial letters at one o'clock in the morning.[47]

[46] Ramsey, p. 64. The period in question is that between 1546 and 1551.

[47] Tawney, *Business and Politics Under James I* (life of Cranfield); Bowen, pp. 413f. The rise of Cranfield is recapitulated in the story of Sir Arthur Ingram, as unfolded in Upton's biography.

In this wakeful dedication to what makes for our benefit, he resembles the French merchant and money-lender, Jacques Coeur (1395?-1456), who comes into the world with nothing, and leaves behind him 300 factories, a palace at Bourges, and houses in Paris and Tours and Montpellier. Jacques Coeur is successful as he grasps the nexus of money and time. He makes his fortune by advancing credit at rates of interest up to 50%. It is not true, what Pound the unhappy revenant supposes, that "with usura hath no man a house of good stone." Interest on capital is in the foundation. The broker or banker advances the capital: at Prato in the fourteenth century, Francesco Datini; at Augsburg in the fifteenth—as the golden tide flows north and westward—Ulrich Fugger; at London in the sixteenth, Sir Thomas Gresham. The magnitude of the usury by which these men engross their fortunes is the measure of the time for which credit is extended. The time is no longer free.

The units of time are estimated more narrowly, as the value of time is computed in monetary terms. In Nuremberg in the sixteenth century, the clocks begin to strike the quarter-hours.[48] The creditor or time-conscious man, who announces the modern age, is notably alert to the striking of the clock. Often this creditor charges no interest; he does not wish to fall foul of the Statute of Usury. Only he stipulates, like Shylock, a very punctual return of the money he advances. "Let him look to his bond." As the borrower is deficient in the sense of time, he is obligated, like the Earl of Norfolk, to pay down, for a loan of 100 pounds, properties worth more than half that sum per annum; or, like Lord Cobham, to

[48] E. Fromm, *Escape from Freedom*, p. 58.

redeem his debt in a ratio of almost 10 to 1.[49] So fruitful is the union of money and time. Now the medieval commonplace, which denies the productivity of money, is exploded. *Pecunia pecuniam non parere potest.*[50] "Nothing will come of nothing." That is what the poet thinks. The usurious man knows better.

"How grievous is the sin of usury," says the medieval Cistercian von Heisterbach (1180?-1240?). In a *Dialog of Miracles,* he recalls with some complacency exemplary stories of moneylenders devoured by reptiles or driven naked through the city and beaten with rods. To the medieval monk, in his naïveté, money that breeds is all-consuming. At last it eats up itself.[51] That is how Aquinas and the Schoolmen conceive it. A contract of mutual risk is permitted, in which the lender may share in the borrower's profit; but that is on the proviso that the lender and the borrower share the risk of loss. There is as yet no thought of that modern innovation, the contract of fixed return. It is not open to the money lender to demand a fixed rate of interest on the stipulated day.

> For when did friendship take
> A breed of barren metal of his friend?

That is, however, the old-fashioned psychology. The rhetorician Thomas Wilson bespeaks it. Wilson thinks that to lop off every "usurers heade in Englande" would constitute "a greater good deede to this lande, than ever was doone by killinge of wolves."[52] His yearning trea-

---

[49] Stone, "Elizabethan Aristocracy," pp. 22-24.

[50] R. Ehrenberg, *Capital & Finance,* p. 21.

[51] Bk. ii, Ch. viii, xxxii, xxxiii, xxxiv. Medieval condemnations of usury are collected in B. N. Nelson, *Idea of Usury,* pp. 3-28.

[52] Preface to *Usury,* written in 1569 and dedicated to Leicester.

tise is obsolete on the day of its publication in 1572, a year after the ban on usury is repealed.

In less progressive times, the approval of Scripture is the portion of those who lend "freely riche and poore Without all gaine of usury."[53] This seems to Calvin an exiguous portion; and so he sanctions the contract of fixed return.[54] Early in the sixteenth century, the Catholic reformer Johann Eck, who is indifferent to the romantic Christianity of the Schoolmen, goes to Bologna (at the expense of the banking house of Fugger) to defend this new contract against the old arrangement based on mutual risk. The Papacy is sympathetic: by the middle of the century, the successors of St. Peter the fisherman of Galilee are spending more than half their income to satisfy interest assessed at fixed rates.[55] In the next century an unregenerate Lutheran, arguing plaintively against the teachings of Martin Bucer, who thinks it legal to put out money at 12%, wants to know "what has become of the book Dr. Luther of blessed memory addressed to the ministers on the subject of usury?"[56] But that is pious nostalgia.

Luther himself, to whom interest is the Devil's invention and "undoubtedly the greatest misfortune of the German nation," is aware that the battle against it has been decided. The "big world-eaters," who are "the covetous man and the usurer," feed without let. Then

[53] *Court of Virtue*, N6.

[54] For Calvin's role in the countenancing of usury, see Nelson, *Idea*, Ch. iii. Melanchthon, Zwingli, and most of all Martin Bucer, are agreeable to a more "liberal" construction of the Biblical prohibition (Nelson, Ch. ii).

[55] Bainton, *Reformation*, p. 248.

[56] N. O. Brown, *Life Against Death*, p. 230.

follows a phrase which encapsulates all the future: "Money," asserts Luther, "is the word of the Devil, through which he creates all things, the way God created through the true word."[57]

In England, the supersession of the old by the new takes a little longer. It is not until the second half of the sixteenth century, and after much backing and filling, that the charging of interest on capital is legalized once and for all:[58] and with the result that money and time become indissolubly one. A more vivid awareness of mortality is sequential. In the golden world, men fleet the time carelessly. But money is time. The opportunity to garner this tangible equivalent is abridged. Anciently, truth is represented as the daughter of time. So the familiar *topos, Veritas filia temporis.* On the more poignant understanding of modern or post-medieval man, the daughter of time is death. The preacher, like the poet but with a different end in view, adjures his parishioners to seize the time. The injunction is hopeful; it is also devoid of hope. Work, says the preacher, for "a diligent hand maketh rich." But now the other face of the injunction: Work, for the night is coming!

Insistently, in the lyric poetry of the Elizabethans, the cruel hand of Death is synonymous with Time's fell hand, which burns the long-lived phoenix and blunts the lion's paws. Time wrinkles as Death dissolves

---

[57] Brown, pp. 220f.; Nelson, p. 32. But Luther, who is initially a literalist in his reading of the Deuteronomic prohibition of usury, is subsequently more complaisant (or timorous) on this issue (Nelson, pp. 44-56).

[58] 10% allowed in 1545; this permission revoked, in consequence of the "great and open usury daily used and practised," in 1552. Legalizing made final in 1571.

the beauty of the fairest brow. Pride, that flowers with the love of things, "Short Time" cuts down with his consuming sickle, or Death assails with arrow, knife, and lance.[59] The theme of transitoriness is the common property of all poets in all ages. The morbid fascination with death, and the melancholy that attends it, are coeval with the beginnings of the modern age.[60]

The medieval maker works as if a thousand years were before him; but also as if he were going to die to-morrow. In the modern age, as the nexus of money and time is confirmed, the coordinate clauses are severed. What remains to the artist is the perplexing image of swift-footed Time. Lincoln Cathedral, in its successive avatars, is two centuries in building; Selby Abbey even longer. The bronze doors of the Baptistery in Florence, at which Ghiberti begins to work early in the fifteenth century, are not completed until half a century later. Except for the statues that stand before Or San Michele, and a small number of other and minor achievements, that is what Lorenzo Ghiberti leaves behind him. Two pairs of doors, wrought in contempt of the passage of years, suffice for the work of a lifetime.

Ghiberti is the type of the old-fashioned maker, but not because he makes comparatively little. Fra Angelico, who is his exact contemporary, is a prolific painter; his

[59] Shakespeare, Sonnet 19; Daniel, *Delia*, 31; Spenser, *FQ*, VIII, vi; C. Schaar, *Motif of Death*, pp. 16f., quoting Turberville and Lord Vaux. Schaar, pp. 10-15, traces the connection in Renaissance poetry of the idea of death and the theme of transitoriness.

[60] "In no period of history, even including the Middle Ages, did the writers feel more conscious of or brood more upon the inevitability of death than in the Renaissance"; Clements "Condemnation of the Poetic Profession," p. 215; he illustrates from emblem literature.

art is, however, like Ghiberti's, covetous of perfection, vastly patient in execution. In the work of these fifteenth-century artists, the note of urgency is conspicuously absent.

Now suddenly the sands are felt as fleeing through the glass. The usurer tells the time, minute by minute. But so does his putative opponent, who is the moralist or clergyman. "Time flyeth away apace, and therfore we are commanded to redeeme the time": Henry Crosse, in his critique of the theatre.[61] The injunction reverberates. Recreation is not blameless, Dudley Fenner supposes, as "we are commaunded, to redeeme the time."[62] Among the directions to the good life set down by the preacher Robert Hill, this occurs: "That with al care I redeeme the time, knowing I shall answere for every idle houre."[63] Even the gentlewoman is exhorted, as by Richard Brathwait, to "eye then your Houre-glasse, vie in teares with graines of sand."[64] Savor the wine "distilling through the limbeck of thy tongue and larynx, and suck the delicious juice of fishes, the marrow of the laborious ox"; but hasten! cries Jeremy Taylor, for the "number of thy days of darkness and the grave cannot be told."[65]

The artist is open to censure, as he squanders precious time on his inutile productions. He responds to the new and more strident censure of his craft by imputing to these productions the power to transcend mortality and time.

[61] *Vertues Common-wealth*, Q2. [62] *Recreations*, A6.
[63] *Pathway*, R4. [64] *English Gentlewoman*, p. 9.
[65] Quoted Herschel Baker, *The Wars of Truth*, p. 63.

'Gainst death and all oblivious enmity
Shall you pace forth; your praise shall still find room
Even in the eyes of all posterity
That wear this world out to the ending doom.

It is, however, the consciousness of time's wasting, more than the perdurable monument, that dominates in these verses of the sixteenth and seventeenth centuries. The minutes are fraught with value, that toil sequentially to their end. Admonishing the poet, possessing his imagination, is the spectre of Time, that gives and confounds his gift in an instant. The plays and poems of Shakespeare are full of time's inexorable progress; the dial hand, ever-moving, is a constant image in the sonnet cycles of Sidney and Spenser and Samuel Daniel. Ralegh broods on Time's consuming rage; Marvell is conscious of Time's shadow; Faustus dies in that shadow, imploring Time to have a stop.

The poet Sir John Denham (1615-1669), known to his contemporaries at Trinity College, Oxford as a "slow and dreaming young man . . . given more to cards and dice than his study," has little to do with the mottoes on sundials. The rise of a House of Fugger, bankers to the Hapsburgs and descendants of a weaver of Graeben, is not accomplished without reference to them.

The Noumenal World and
the Torrent of Change

WHEN PLATO attacks poetry, and notably in Book III of the *Republic*, it is the slow and dreaming young man who bears the brunt of his contempt. In the poet, who daffs the world aside, the claims of business are dishonored. Poetry is an imitative art, which requires of its adepts uncommon dedication. But no man can be an adept in all things: "one man can only do one thing well, and not many" (394E). It follows that "the same person will hardly be able to play a serious part in life, and at the same time be an imitator" (395A): by definition, one who cultivates the arts.

The argument recurs frequently in the polemical literature of the Renaissance. Poetry belongs to the interstices of things. Although, in this literature, the bias of the early Fathers is always perceptible, the critical debt is to Plato, whose tutelage is apparent everywhere in the attack on poetry and the theatre. That is, perhaps, another way of asserting that the Fathers themselves are platonic. What St. Jerome says of Philo Judaeus might be said as applicably of St. Jerome: "Either Plato philonizes, or Philo platonizes."

But Plato, who denigrates poetry as it separates a man and his business, is not always at one in defining this business with the platonizers of the Renaissance. The platonic critique is superficially utilitarian, and so associates its author with the party of progress. But appearances, as Plato is concerned to argue elsewhere, are notoriously deceiving. In fact Plato is explicitly hostile to progress. The Age of Pericles, like England in the dawn of the Enlightenment, is profoundly optimistic. This welling up of good hope, as it is founded on temporal achievement, seems to Plato crudely eupeptic. In his deprecatory psychology, he resembles unexpectedly his natural antagonist, the mournful Sophocles, indicting the insolent ambition of imperialistic Athens in the central stasimon of *Oedipus the King*.[1] His own antecedents, to whom he is faithful as a commentator on society, are of the landholding or conservative class.[2] The mercantile democracy of the fifth century and later, in which the expanding economies of the Renaissance are augured, is only, as he conceives it, the cheap occasion of the "heaping up of riches," which "beats to the same tune" as illiberality and meanness (*Laws*, Bk. v). His prejudice against money-breeding and the possessors of moveable goods leads him to number "among dishonorable things" whatever "relates to retail trade and merchandise" (xi). The ideal city, he thinks, must have among its inhabitants "as few as possible of the retail class" (xi) and those who follow "the vulgar trade which is carried on by lending money" (v). In this city, "no gold or silver Plutus shall dwell" (v). Believing that "the care of riches should have the last place in our thoughts" and that "the possession of great wealth is of no use" except as it "makes the soul brag-

---

[1] Ll. 863-911; B. Knox, *Oedipus at Thebes*, pp. 99ff.
[2] Discussion draws on A. Winspear, *The Genesis of Plato's Thought*, pp. 161, 163, 305.

103

gart and insolent" (v), he seeks to protect his Utopia against mercantile corruption by locating it not less than ten miles from the sea (iv). But the poet and the merchant are each, in their different ways, the connoisseurs of temporalities. It is for this reason that each is under ban.

The platonic critique can hardly have seemed comfortable to the acidulated writer of the sixteenth and seventeenth centuries, who objects to the theatre on utilitarian grounds. But the appeal to use does not always envisage the "heaping up of riches." Often it is a rallying point for the disaffected man, and serves to focus his sense of estrangement. Plato in his own time is very much a man apart, whose quarrel with society is momentous for the history of thought. It is the livid fact of this quarrel—not the social philosophy but the cry of pain—that suggests his intimate relation to the poet-haters of the Renaissance.

Plato, who grows to manhood in a period of cataclysmic change, is the classic type of the revenant who verges on despair and, as he is cunning, finds an alternative. The distinction he enforces, between the way of truth and the way of opinion, is a sheet anchor thrown out against chaos. As he denigrates whatever is palpable and mutable, he fulfills the austere tendencies of the earlier Pythagoreans, to whom the body is a clog, and the Eleatic philosophers like Parmenides and Zeno, whose defensive concern is to elaborate a static and ideal world in which change and multiplicity—the province of the body—are seen to be illusions. The testimony of the senses is deceptive. The arrow never flies, nor can

Achilles overtake the tortoise. "Forever wilt thou love, and she be fair!"

But Plato, who fulfills the past, is also a prophet. He is the great exemplar of those displaced and frenetic persons whose number is legion in the later sixteenth century, and who, exactly as they float upon a wild and violent sea, affirm the presence of immutable law: like Edmund Spenser, the angry satirist of *Mother Hubberds Tale*, who identifies change with economic and ecclesiastical abuses and seeks to cancel it altogether in the final cantos of the *Faerie Queene*; or like the rhetorician Thomas Wilson, who contemplates unhappily a country swayed by "the meanest sort . . . in which everything is permitted to all," and whose passionate conviction it is that "the world is not governed by wisdom or policy, but by a secret purpose or fatal destiny."[3]

Fatum regit mundum: the flux is denied. The abstract edifice which is Plato's enduring monument is conceived, like Wilson's ideal commonwealth or like the frozen world of Spenser's poem, not in expectancy but in revulsion. It is the triumph of desire over the fact. This edifice is powerful for good as it overtops the Syracusan debacle and the discrediting of Plato's own conservative and oligarchic party: at home, the defeat of the Thirty; abroad, the failure of Dion's restoration. "Shall I tell you then what we ought to do and what justice requires?" (Epistle II, 312a)[4]

---

[3] Wilson quoted in Tawney's edition of *Usury*, p. 15. For the coexistence in Spenser of moderate reformism and an almost hysterical appeal to a happier and more settled past, see Holden, *Anti-Puritan Satire*, pp. 86-93.

[4] Possibly a spurious letter; the sentiment is, however, sufficiently canonical.

The millenarian of the seventeenth century—Colonel
Harrison, Colonel Goffe—invokes the same require-
ments. Ideal justice is pitted against the unassimilable
(or merely historical) fact. John Owen, the dissenting
minister whom Cromwell appoints vice-chancellor of
Oxford, is prone to dejection as he sees how the faithful
are harried. "The summer is ended, and the harvest is
past, and we are not refreshed." Cromwell himself, who
expects the day of the Lord and fails to find it, is ready
to cry out in his misery, "Oh, would I had wings like
a dove."[5] But the resort in either case is not to flight. It is
to asseveration, and a repudiating of the testimony of the
senses. Owen is sure that God is not working "for this
or that form of government or civil administration of
human affairs." His abiding concern, the apparent course
of events notwithstanding, "is *that Zion may be found-
ed*, and the general interest of all the sons and daughters
of Zion be preserved." Cromwell, as the Spirit of God
is strong upon him, looks quite through the physical
world. Often the requirements of justice are vitiated by
the promptings of the flesh. Cromwell is indifferent to
these promptings. "I would not," he announces, "con-
sult flesh and blood."[6]

Justice is temporarily ascendant, even in historical
time. Sparta is victorious in the Peloponnesian War
(the church of visible saints is established). That is an
earnest of beneficent change. But the successes of Sparta,
which also contemns the merchant and makes a fetish of
self-denial, are transitory successes. Spartan power dis-

[5] Simpson, *Puritanism*, pp. 91, 93.
[6] Simpson, pp. 71, 85 (Cromwell, determining on the execution
of the King).

106

integrates at Leuctra (371 BC): one senses the work-
ings of inevitable process; the rising power of Mace-
donia supervenes. Always,

> The present pleasure,
> By revolution lowering, does become
> The opposite of itself.

It is the happiness of William Bradford, the historian
of the Plymouth Plantation, to see in his first times the
blessed fruits of the sweet communion of saints. But
fidelity decays and ruin approaches. Inexorably, the
subtle serpent untwists the sacred bonds. Governor Brad-
ford, who precedes Cromwell in death by only a year,
dies, like the Protector, a disappointed man. The failure
of the New Israel, which he laments and bewails in his
age, is, however, a predictable failure. "And for others
warning and admonition, and my own humiliation, do
I here note the same."[7]

All earthly foundations are necessarily abandoned.
Zion is invested, at Massachusetts Bay, subsequently in
Rhode Island. To flee to the periphery of civilized life,
like the Anabaptists, is unavailing. So with the retreat
to the wilderness. The haven for religious refugees
which Roger Williams had thought to establish at Provi-
dence is degraded, as the wheels turns, to a source of
profit-taking for the rich. "The common trinity of the
world—Profit, Preferment, Pleasure"—is there "the
tria omnia, as in all the world besides."[8] The remedy
is to look beyond the temporal world, to proclaim a dis-
tinction between the world of nature and the world of
grace—in platonic terms, to distinguish pure form from

[7] Simpson, pp. 33f.   [8] Williams quoted in Simpson, p. 59.

107

its superficial manifestations. Plato, who appeals from the random spinning of the wheel to the deification of unchanging form, is like the baffled millenarian of the later seventeenth century: for example, Richard Baxter, in whom despair unexpectedly gives way to elation, as he decides that human history is not finally to the point. In historical time, the night is longer than the day; the day itself is torn with storms and tempests.[9] This dreary chronicle is indited, however, in the language of opinion; over against it is set the language of truth—not the triumph of the Elizabethan Settlement or the Restoration of Belial: or the vaunting of immorality in stage plays, but the miracle of rebirth in the Lord.

The perpetual synod of saints is deferred, like the Rule of the Thirty. But good hope is not deferred; only it is translated. There is no necessity, Baxter thinks, to expect great matters of the Church (or State) on earth, or to dream of a golden age or kingdom of this world. The religious enthusiast, who has escaped from time, is richer in the possession of "the faith that overcometh the world."[10] This faith is superior to temporal consolations, like the sensuous music of the poet. That is the strength and center of the platonic critique. Plato in the *Republic*, as he denies the here and now, anticipates the true or willful believer, after the collapse of the covenanted community. On this side, the *Republic* resembles and anticipates the *City of God*, which Augustine composes in response to the sack of Rome and the failure of all trust in temporal things; or it is analogous

[9] Baxter in Simpson, p. 98.
[10] John Wesley, in his rules for the communion of saints; quoted in Simpson, p. 105.

108

to the ascetic labors and reproaches of St. Jerome, after the shattering triumph of the Goths at Adrianople.

The better world envisaged by Plato is located in time. In this it differs ostensibly from the heavenly city. In the future is the Promised Land, when the saints shall inherit the earth. The millenarian or platonic philosopher anticipates this temporal inheritance. But the apocalyptic view of history he endorses, like the eschatological view of Augustine, means essentially the repudiating of history—phenomenal fact, the days of darkness—in favor of a quasi-religious act of faith.

Intimations of religious conversion are heard, in Plato's preferring to crass mundaneity the keener pleasures of the noumenal world. Plato, arriving in Sicily as tutor to young Dion, the son-in-law of the King, is like Saul on the road to Damascus; or he is like Augustine coming to Carthage, "where there sang all around me a cauldron of unholy loves." Upon his arrival, he finds himself repelled by the abandonment in time and sense of the coarser Italians, who make it a rule "to avoid all industry except such as is devoted to banquets and drinking bouts and painstaking attention to the gratification of lust" (Epistle vii, 326d). He turns from this gross and evanescent existence to the creating of a morbid *hortus inclusus,* in which time must have a stop. One thinks of the seventeenth-century preacher, who revolts at the excesses of "the brats of Babylon," and determines "to give God no rest till he sets up Jerusalem as the praise of the whole world."[11]

But this utopian city which the visionary announces is tainted—like the Bible to the Antinomian soldier—

[11] Simpson, pp. 76f.

precisely as it is of the world. In the platonic Utopia, sense is refined or it is purged. The rocky surface, which endures without change, takes precedence over the plain, which bears its fruit and dies.[12] But even the rock is subject to mortality. And so Plato looks deeper, to discover those laws which are impervious to the abrading power of time. He finds them in geometry, which is a "knowledge of the eternal, and not of aught perishing and transient" (*Republic*, VII, 527B). His resort to the constant formulae of mathematics, like the resort of the true believer to an immaterial covenant of grace, enables him to coerce the torrent of material change. Stasis describes the mathematical world, from which the female principle, which fructifies but only for a little, is necessarily excluded. In this world, the odd, as it balances extremes between a middle term, is preferred to the even, which is itself alone. Of curved figures, only the circle, returning again to its point of departure and so fulfilling a perfect round, is admitted. But the demotic language which is poetry is not admitted. Its commitment is to the flux.

The iconoclast of the sixteenth and seventeenth centuries desires the interdicting of poetry. Plato, in spirit, sanctions the mutilating of the Hermae. But the sanctioning does not derive from mere political bias (his supposed adhesion to the conservative party). Politics, like poetry, has to do with the surface of things. This means, it does not serve, or not sufficiently, to rationalize the event. The real impulsion lies deeper. To illustrate, in terms of the sixteenth and seventeenth centuries: Roger

[12] Winspear, p. 333, citing *Laws*.

Williams, as he breaks with the Cottons and Winthrops of Massachusetts, sows the seeds of religious freedom. The occasion of this break is, however, his belief that the authorities are not so alert as they should be to the chasm which separates the elect from the unregenerate man. Richard Baxter, the egalitarian, who argues for tolerance but after the saints have been cast down, is making the best of a bad situation. Baxter in power is sufficiently despotic. To disfranchise the non-believer is only, he supposes, to preserve him from the chance of incurring greater guilt.[13] The Anabaptists of the sixteenth century are fervent apostrophizers of the Naked Truth. As that is so, they are inimical to poetry. This melodramatic sect, which the Marxist historian salutes as epitomizing a more progressive future, enters history partly in consequence of the decline of the medieval *compagnonnages*. As the inundation of precious metals from the mines of America drives down the purchasing power of the currency, the price of basic consumables rises dramatically; and with the result that industry and trade are encouraged to expand and so to shake off the restrictive control of the guilds.[14] The exploitation of the worker follows predictably, and inclines him to look to a better world. As he seeks to found it in the here and now (as under the leadership of Thomas Muenzer), he becomes an emblem of progress: for example, to Friedrich Engels.

Plato, on the other hand, is a kind of reactionary. But as he smashes the icons, he gives a lead to the party of progress in the Renaissance; and even though the po-

[13] Simpson, quoting Baxter, p. 96.
[14] Ramsey, *Tudor Economic Problems*, pp. 116, 120.

litical prepossessions of that party differ absolutely from his own. The two are one in first and last things. That is why the platonic critique is congenial to the dispossessed fanatic of the sixteenth and seventeenth centuries as well as to the merchant who engineers his misery. Each is marked by *parti pris*. "I want money," says Aristippus; "Plato wants books." The poetic intelligence, and the kind of temperament which quickens to the language of poetry, is indifferent to the consolations of endemic form, as to that crasser security which preoccupies the genus Thorowgood.

The business of the scribbler whom the alderman keeps in his pocket to write against the stage is to see that money-making goes forward without interruption. The more conventional polemicist, who denounces poetry and the theatre, is not so disingenuous. Edmund Rudierde detests the playwright but also the usurer.[15] This impartial confounding is apparent in the strictures of George Wither and the parliamentarian and preacher Francis Rous. In Thomas Lupton's Utopia, the theatre has no place: and "every one that shal borrow money upon Usury the thirde time . . . shall suffer death."[16] Lupton, who is not so remorseless as Plato, is willing to spare the usurious man who makes a clean breast. Only "he shal have his right hande cut off."

This dual condemnation appears to invalidate a simplistic reading of the war against poetry. The impulse to self-aggrandizement is indubitable; but it is not the single key. Here, from Blackstone's *Commentaries* (1766), is an illustration of the compendious or simplis-

[15] *Thunderbolt*, pp. 82-85.
[16] *Siuqila*, p. 149.

tic point of view. The prohibition of usury, says the legal historian, is a product of the "Dark Ages," a period of "monkish superstitions and civil tyranny." In this period, "commerce was at its lowest ebb." Capitalism, and its "inseparable companion," the "doctrine of loans upon interest," become possible only as the darkness is routed by the Protestant reformer. It is this reformer who sponsors the "revival of true religion and real liberty."[17]

In these observations, the thesis of Max Weber is already potential.[18] One may summarize, as follows. Usury is interdicted by Scripture.[19] Modern capitalism finds this interdicting disagreeable. The Protestant reformer, as he also is concerned to smooth the road for what pays, sees how to get round the Deuteronomic prohibition. The applicability to poetry is obvious. "To applaud certain qualities"—industry, thrift, material productivity—"is by implication to condemn the habits and institutions which appear to conflict with them."[20] Poetry is an emblem of these habits and institutions. As usury is countenanced for crudely economic reasons, so poetry is discountenanced, for exactly the same reasons, by the businessman and by his allies and servants among the clergy. The people want to know what they must do to be saved. The preacher instructs them to "trust in Jesus Christ and put on the whole armor of God." But this instruction, which entails the putting away of idle poetry, has in view another or more complicated end than

---

[17] *Commentaries*, Bk. ii, Ch. xxx; quoted in Nelson, *Idea*, p. 108.
[18] *The Protestant Ethic and the Spirit of Capitalism.*
[19] Deuteronomy 23:19 disallows the charging of interest within the group. But the group is the world, since, as St. Thomas and other medieval commentators suppose, all men are brothers.
[20] R. H. Tawney, *Religion and the Rise of Capitalism*, p. 251.

113

salvation in the life to come: "behind the thinning veil of doctrine and image the Puritan Revolution was gathering momentum."[21]

This thesis is plausible, and finds considerable support in the literature of tracts and sermons—which also requires its drastic modification. Tawney, who is sometimes belittled by his inferiors as he locates in Calvinism the creed and justification of a new commercial *régime*, is at pains to establish the economic conservatism of the Protestant reformers. "Like some elements in the Catholic reaction of the twentieth century, the Protestant reaction of the sixteenth sighed for a vanished age of peasant prosperity. The social theory of Luther, who hated commerce and capitalism, has its nearest modern analogy in the Distributive State of Mr. Belloc and Mr. Chesterton."[22] The typical reformer expects the "imminent desolation, or conclusive dissolution of this foolish doting worlde," as he finds it universally—in the theatre but in the counting house as well—"an indigested Chaos of outragious enormities." He is, par excellence, the uprooted hysteric. In the Court, he thinks, "the Nobility are hardly distinguisht from their followers: in City, the Merchant is not known from his Factor: in Country, the Gentry cannot be descried or described from the Bacon-eating, brawny-handed Rustick ... there is scarce any difference betwixt Countesse and Curtezan, Lady and Chamber-maid, Mistresse and greasy Kitchen-wench, Gentleman and Mechanicke." But the best the moralist can do, in rationalizing the

[21] W. Haller, *Rise of Puritanism*, p. 51.
[22] *Religion and the Rise of Capitalism*, p. 101. And see pp. 98-102, 215-18, 224.

event, is to point with inchoate anger to "that garish Strumpet, PRIDE." He concludes, like the ribald gentleman in Shakespeare's play but with a different animus altogether, "as for Knight and Tailor, there goes but a paire of Sheares betwixt them."[23]

As this old-fashioned man is not remarkable for prescience or self-consciousness, the writing he sponsors is significant intrinsically, only as the stuff of a disconcerting chapter in the history of bad ideas. He impinges on history, as he is used. The coming together in the Protestant reformer of religious radicalism and economic conservatism is efficient in ways unintended and unforeseen by this agitated person. "What, therefore, is important for us to understand is less how learned doctors argued among themselves than what they succeeded in conveying to the people, not what their doctrine was but what it meant and did" (William Haller).[24]

The perplexed and obscure poet Robert Anton, who sets out to "scourge and correct" the theatre (among a host of dissimilar abuses), is not assisting by design at the birth of a society more circumspect in dealing with time and money. He wonders uneasily at women, who are

[23] *This Worlds Folly*, B4v, A3v.

[24] P. 86. It is this kind of insight that seems to me to constitute the chief merit of the Weber thesis. Compare the following passage from *The Protestant Sects and the Spirit of Capitalism* (in H. H. Gerth and C. Wright Mills, *From Max Weber*, p. 321): "it is not the ethical *doctrine* of a religion . . . that matters," but the conduct of the religious man. In the case of the Puritan, this conduct "paved the way for the 'spirit' of modern capitalism." And see Tawney, *Religion*, p. 225: "The fundamental question, after all, is not what kind of rules a faith enjoins, but what type of character it esteems and cultivates."

growne so mad,
That their immodest feete like planets gad
With such irregular motion to base Playes,
Where all the deadly sinnes keepe hollidayes.[25]

But this madness is pervasive. In the new society or "iron age" that is preparing, as the displaced man asserts in a dedication to William Herbert, the Earl of Pembroke, "the sects of vice are more than in Amsterdam." His reaction is not to look to the future, like Bacon the optimist and progressive, but to a more settled and explicable past. "What marvell is it," asks Bacon's less hopeful contemporary, the poet William Vaughan, that "wee praise the old, and hate the present time?"[26]

It is the more cursory eye of hindsight which sees under one aspect the affectation of piety in the banning of plays by the elders of Stratford-upon-Avon (1612), men who are loyal only to their bread: and the disinterested bigotry of the Puritan preacher who construes the *Practise of Christianitie* as prohibiting our pleasure in the stage; or which infers that the Puritan theologian, who spurns at plays and romances under the heading "abominations," in the *True Watch and Rule of Life* (1622), is commending the more aggressive watch and rule his indictment helps to initiate. The Reverend Richard Rogers, though he denounces the players as "unprofitable caterpillers" who are "burdensome and chargeable to others," allows "no place to that common Oppression in the world by lending, which is called usury; or any other seeking of a man's private profit."[27] John

[25] *Vices Anotimie*, 1617, 13v.
[26] *Spirit of Detraction*, 1611, p. 348.
[27] *Practise of Christianitie*, 1618 ed., pp. 404, 211.

Brinsley, who sees the concourse of players as bringing "fagots and fire-brands to set in the gates of our Jerusalem," also entertains a more generalized horror of "the new guise of sundry . . . to corrupt all the hope and glory of our Land." Mostly, he is distraught that we have "left off the searching of the holy booke of God, which unto our Fathers was much dearer than their lives."[28] It is the faith of our fathers that is uppermost here. Like Mr. Hardcastle, these are men who love everything that's old. Unhappily for their affections and intentions, the sum of what they write is subversive of the old. As they are hunting the past in the present, they take hands with Bounderby and Gradgrind, whose reason for being is to bury the past.

In the protest of the poet Hesiod against painted poetry (*Theogony*, ll. 26-28), political considerations are decisive, only in the second place. Hesiod recalls nostalgically that Saturnian age when men "lived like gods without sorrow of heart . . . and had all good things," and when the "earth unforced bare them fruit abundantly and without stint" (*Works and Days*, 109ff.). But with the dislocating of the old pastoral life, apparent chaos emerges: "earth is full of evils and the sea is full," and "now truly is a race of iron, and men never rest from labour and sorrow . . . and the gods . . . lay sore trouble upon them" (ll. 101, 176ff.). The conventional poet—Homer, for example—offers no palliative to these emerging evils. His poetry is involved with the fluid world of phenomena. It is against this world that the abstracting psychology, bred of rootlessness and discontent, enters its protest. Compare Plato, in the *Laws*,

[28] *True Watch and Rule*, pp. 302, 228.

117

remembering the old days before the deluge, when "there was no great poverty; nor was poverty a cause of difference among men; and rich they could not be, if they had no gold and silver." In this pristine time, adherence is to "the noblest principles; there is no insolence or injustice, nor . . . any contentions or envyings."

> And therefore men were good . . . for what they heard of the nature of good and evil in their simplicity they believed to be true, and practised. No one had the wit to suspect another of a falsehood, as men do now; but what they heard about Gods and men they believed to be true, and lived accordingly . . . [a life] simpler and more manly, and also more temperate and in general more just (Bk. III).

Hesiod in the eighth century, celebrating "the ever-sure foundation of all" (*Theogony*, l. 117), adumbrates this yearning and retrospective psychology. The Orphics in the next century (like the early Christians), as they represent the dispossessed at the bottom of society, pit the everlasting One against its phenomenal and discouraging exemplifications. The Pythagoreans and Eleatics, and later Socrates and Plato, extend this opposition; but not as they speak for the poorer peasant or the worker but for the conservative oligarch whose day is also passing. In each case, the end is to hypothesize a more stable existence, safe from the depredations of chance and social change.

The miscellany writer John Hall, who invokes on profane poetry the vengeance of the old Hebraic God, entertains no bright vision of a new day preparing, when the business of everyman will be business. The invertebrate anger which disfigures his homilies is reserved for a time when "usury is witty winning," and the subtle merchant is identified by "gredy gaine of gold."[29] As this hysterical writer is compelled to abide a ceaseless and often a contradictory disarranging of long-settled ways and forms, he epitomizes nicely the waif in an age of change for whom an equable existence is precluded. The result is frustration, which engenders despair and finds its solvent in acrimony and violence. This violence must discover an object against which it can beat (those others, those caterpillars!), lest it turn on its host and destroy him. That is why the history of the earlier Tudors rings with alarms and excursions, while that of their successors is poisoned with invective: the heroic folly of the Pilgrimage of Grace, or the rebellion of the younger Wyatt, or the penning of the Marprelate tracts. In our time, says the homilist (it might be old Gloucester, in *King Lear*):

> what devouring Plagues, what Fires, what Inundations, what unseasonable Seasons, what prodigious Births, what unnatural Meteors, what malevolent Conjunctions, what ominous Apparitions, what bloudy assassinations of mighty Kings, what Rapes, what Murthers, what fraudulencies betwixt Brother and Brother? what horrible Conspiracies by Sonnes against Fathers.[30]

The religion to which the homilist or the rebel adheres, whether Protestant or Catholic, does not matter so much as the consuming need he feels for recognizable contours. This need is apparent in his stridency, as in his vain attempt to restore the old order before the

---

[29] *Court of Virtue*, B4, VI.　　[30] *This Worlds Folly*, C1-v.

119

flood. "How long then," he demands of the Creator, "wilt Thou forget to be just? Oh, how long wilt Thou shut up the vesselles of Thy wrath, and protract revenge?"[31] Revolution is implicit in this summons to revenge. But the revolutionary, as often, is a pawn. He is not a friend of the new men who are soon to dominate society and make it over in their image.[32] It appears to him that Hell is not more odious than England in the early years of Elizabeth's reign: when covetousness takes precedence of all other sins, and private wealth is preferred to commonwealth: when no man walks in his proper vocation, and "a lowte with a lorde will proudely checkmate." Of course he wrings his hands as the sumptuary laws are flouted, and especially by women ("Eche lasse like a lady is clothed in silke"). That is as he remembers how it was "when I was a boy."[33]

It is worth comparing the imprecations of Thomas Carlyle, in another time of unrest and dislocation: "The Sumptuary Laws have fallen into such a state of desue-

[31] B4v-C.

[32] For the "reactionary" character of much Protestant protest, and its emphatic rejection of usury and economic malpractice, see C. and K. George, *Protestant Mind*, pp. 148-59, 166-69. The "tone of Calvinist opinion regarding the social and psychological realities of early English capitalism" is "essentially conservative, angry, and frightened" (p. 160). There is "no significant positive correlation between the philosophy of the bourgeoisie *qua* bourgeosie and the religious idealism of Protestantism. There is certainly no evidence of dynamic, psychological, causal connection between Calvinism and either Weberian capitalism or the far more significant capitalism of 'this worldly' predation" (p. 173). The latter statement seems to me too strong; nonetheless, it is a useful corrective to the point of view which hypothesizes a one-to-one correspondence between the new society and the new religion.

[33] *Court of Virtue*, z.v.ᵛ.

tude as was never before seen."[34] I think this state of desuetude was disquieting to Hindenburg also. "Our city," as Plato laments in his age, "was no longer guided by the customs and practices of our fathers, while to train up new ones was anything but easy. And the corruption of our written laws and our customs was proceeding at such amazing speed that . . . when I noted these changes and saw how unstable everything was, I became in the end quite dizzy" (Epistle vii, 325e).

What is primary in these maledictions is a vastly disagreeable understanding that "the fashion is changed."[35] This understanding enforces the detestation of painted poetry, which is felt as untrue precisely because it is inconstant. "Waver no more with every winde but once cleave to a constant minde": that is the redactor of secular verse, employing the form against the content.[36]

The sequence is familiar. First Gracchus Babeuf and then the 18th Brumaire; first Robert Applegarth and then the TUC. In the beginning, poetry is attacked as corrosive of civic virtue. It is "like a sincke in a towne, whereunto all the filth doth runne: or a bile in the body, that draweth all the ill humours to it." Then follows the capitulation of civic virtue: the prevalence of "cosonage and buying and selling" and the empery of the merchant, who "for a private gaine, will murmur at a common good." Henry Crosse, who draws up this indictment even as he assails the stage and popular poetry as purveying so many "legends of Lies," would not have supposed the title of his volume—he calls it Virtue's Commonwealth, or the Highway to Honor—descriptive

[34] *Past and Present*, Bk. iii, Ch. xiii.
[35] *Court of Virtue*, z.v.ᵛ.   [36] M4-v.

121

of that commonwealth whose advent he hastens. In the iron age he hypothesizes, vice rides on horseback. "It is not the riches of Cressus," he advises the Lord Mayor and Aldermen of London, to whom his poisonous tract is directed, "can make a man truly happy, or crowne him with true honour, but onely Vertue."[37]

No doubt Mayor Lee and his brethren were willing to assent to this pious proposition. The moralist does not look very hard at the revolution these leaders of society are in process of accomplishing. He is off on his hobby horse, raving against cosmetics (faces slubbered "with so many ointments and dregs"), or imputing to the Devil the invention of starch. The passing of the old order rouses him to frenzy. Take but degree away, and "every base Tapster or Oastler will be as fine as a Gentleman."[38] Given his angry confusion, he is a dreadful hammer in the hands of more forward-looking men, who pledge the dead past in the words of Ancient Pistol: "for, lambkins, we will live!"

[37] *Vertues Common-wealth*, H4v, I2, K2v-3, D2v.
[38] K4-v, L1.

VI Politics and Poetry

THE COLLISION of past and present goes far to explain the enduring quarrel over the stage between the Crown and the City, as represented in the Privy Council and the London Corporation.[1] In the beginning the actor, like the beggar, is defined as a vagrant; the City Fathers seek to move him along. Or else the actor, as he causes unruly crowds to assemble, gives occasion to riot or pilfering or plague. When, however, a reforming bishop of London requests of Mr. Secretary Cecil that plays be banned in the City so long as the plague is raging, the grin of hate shows through in the parenthetical remark: "and if it were for ever, it were not amiss" (Edmund Grindal, 1563).

The wish begets the deed. In the years just before the first public theatre is constructed, the Lord Mayor determines to evict the players once and for all. The Privy Council demurs (1572). To emphasize its support of the drama, it confers a patent royal on Lord Leicester's Servants, who are privileged to ignore the ban on theatrical entertainments (1574). The Corporation rejoins by requiring a license of every play performed within

---

[1] The quarrel is recapitulated in Chambers, *Elizabethan Stage*, I, ix; Holden, *Anti-Puritan Satire*, pp. 94-101; and, more succinctly, by S. F. Johnson in *Reader's Encyclopedia of Shakespeare*, pp. 210-12. Chambers, Vol. IV, Appendix D, assembles the pertinent documents.

its jurisdiction. It is a version of the wild goose chase, as Mercutio describes it.[2] A year later, and despite the opposition of the Crown, the Corporation enacts its earlier purpose of expelling all players from the City (1575). The result is, however, unlooked for: the players, removing to the Liberties outside the walls, where the writ of the magistracy ceases to run, draw their patrons by bridge or by water to the Surrey side. As that is so, the amount of time the worker subtracts from his working day is not diminished but increased. The Lord Mayor takes alarm, and addresses a petition to the Lord Chancellor urging that plays be banned in the Liberties also (1580). Northbrooke, in his general anathematizing, seconds this remonstrance. It falls on deaf ears. The Council orders the City to readmit the players (1581, 1582), and even to bestow its favor on the troupe newly organized under Walsingham's aegis and dignified with the portentous title, the Queen's Company. Countermeasures follow, in which the spirit if not the letter of the royal injunction is denied: the posting of play bills is made illegal (1581); the livery companies are instructed to see that their apprentices break off attendance at plays (1582).

The Privy Council, as the organ of the Crown, is not always or altogether partial to the theatre. Its equivocations are, however, a matter of exigency. Though Elizabeth is uneasy at the banning of plays on the Sabbath, and in fact disallows a more restrictive measure commended to her by the Speaker of the House, the

----

[2] The exchange of correspondence between the London Corporation and the Privy Council, together with other "Documents of Control," is given by Chambers, *Elizabethan Stage*, IV, Appendix D.

Council on this head falls in with the demands of the City, and extends the prohibition of Sunday playing in the reign of James and Charles. (The edict goes unenforced.[3]) It agrees, but only formally and therefore to no real purpose, that the public theatres ought to be demolished (1597). When James Burbage attempts to schedule public performances of plays in the old refectory of Blackfriars, he is stayed by a petition addressed to the Crown (1597). But the Council does not prevent his sons from leasing the theatre to a private company, nor does it interfere with their move to the Bankside. The statute of Elizabeth dealing with vagabonds and masterless men is renewed by James I, who is also concerned to enjoin the use in dramatic entertainments of the name of God or Christ or the Holy Ghost or the Trinity (1606). The willingness of playwrights and players to take notice of public grumbling, as in response to the projected marriage of Prince Charles and the Spanish Infanta, is construed as *lèse majesté*, and occasions the prohibiting of "lavish and licentious speech about matters of state" (1620).

The Stuarts are more efficient than their predecessors in exercising the censorship; and that is a fact which tallies nicely with their explicit assumption of the pretensions of divine right. It is the power which has already begun to decay and not the power at its zenith which insists on its own infallibility and is most vigilant in discovering and persecuting dissent.[4] Innocent III,

---

[3] D. Neal, *The History of the Puritans*, I, 176. The Council complains, in 1591, of the flouting of the ban on Sunday performances. Crashaw in 1607 reiterates this complaint, and Prynne in 1633.

[4] F. S. Siebert, *Freedom of the Press*, pp. 10, 108f.

who is really or very nearly sovereign in the temporal sphere as well as in the religious, forbears to lay claim to the keys of civil and spiritual authority; that act of folly is reserved to his feckless successors, the Popes of the Reformation, whose assertion of prerogative grows more shrill as the progress of the great schism belies it. And hence the Court, in the early seventeenth century, undertakes more narrowly than it had a generation before to watch over the stage and to exorcise real or imaginary offenses. But it does not rescind its patronage of plays. On the contrary, the patronage of plays is confirmed.

This patronage, like the rejection of the theatre by its opponents, is a contingent phenomenon. Early in the sixteenth century, Parliament forbids the upper classes to spend more than two shillings on a foreign cap or bonnet (1529). That is legislation which the English craftsman can endorse enthusiastically: he is a patriot and so he is scornful of foreign importations. As this craftsman is protected by the sumptuary laws, his wherewithal increases; nativism goes out the window. A half century later, it is necessary that Parliament require, of the lower classes, the wearing of an English woolen cap on the Sabbath (1570). That is one illustration of the want of a simple or straight-line progression between the effect and the cause. Here is another. Early in the fifteenth century the Florentine banker Giovanni di Bicci finds it expedient to support the *popolani* against the nobility or *grandi*. Amassing a fortune, he leaves it to his sons, who manifest a less turbulent spirit. Cosimo Patriae Pater and Lorenzo the Magnificent, whatever their qualities, are not to be described as democratic.

Nor does their origin in the middle class, which is inclined to philistinism in its estimate of the usefulness of art, prevent them from becoming the greatest of all the great patrons.

The strictures of Wyclif and the draconians who succeed him are absolute; the extreme and more logical position for which they speak is ultimately approved by the greatest number of their adherents, as the instinct grows more imperious "to try decapitation and to play truant from the body bush." But throughout the sixteenth century interludes and moralities, like *New Custom* (1573) or *Lusty Juventus* (*c.* 1550), seek to promote the cause of Reform; and they communicate in its interest the same idiom and spirit as appears in the tirades of William Prynne (who is not hostile to religious plays). Thomas Lupton, who inveighs against the secular drama, writes a pietistic play on the evils of wealth. Theodore Beza, who is, after Calvin, the principal leader of the Reformation in France, is also the author of one of the more popular plays in dramatic history.[5] The dissenting Bishop of Ossory, John Bale, who is threatened with punishment "*ob* [on account of] *editas comedias*," finds a protector in the Lord Chancellor Thomas Cromwell, who is not much remembered for his devotion to plays.[6] It is in the house of Archbishop Cranmer that Bale's *King Johan* (before 1548) is first performed. The play, as it happens, is a virulent attack on Roman Ca-

---

[5] Lupton, *All for Money*, *c.*1578; Beza, *Abraham sacrifiant*, 1550, trans. Golding, 1575.

[6] Bale is threatened by Archbishop Lee in 1534. Chambers, *Elizabethan Stage*, I, 242, sees a deliberate attempt on Cromwell's part to make the stage an engine of Protestant propaganda.

127

tholicism. Cromwell is pleased to hear from a proselyting vicar (Thomas Wylley) that he has "made a play agaynst the popes counseleurs";[7] and Cranmer to receive a dramatic tractate by the German Protestant Thomas Kirchmayer, in which AntiChrist is identified with the Pope.[8] But the play, subsequently, is presented at Cambridge, to the intense displeasure of Bishop Stephen Gardiner, the Roman Catholic Chancellor to the University. Much depends on whose ox is gored.[9]

It is no marvel, says John Foxe in his *Book of Martyrs*, that Gardiner attempts to thwart the players, printers, and preachers: "for he seeth these three things to be set up of God, as a triple bulwark against the triple crown of the Pope." Under Cromwell, the player and preacher raise their voices together in praise of Reform. On the fall of Cromwell, this union is forcibly dissolved. The enemies of Reform, as they return once more to power, vex and trouble "the poore minstrels, and players of enterludes." Bale discloses the ground of this renewed persecution. So long as the players "played lyes, and sange baudy songes, blasphemed God, and corrupted men's consciences, ye never blamed them. . . . But sens they persuaded the people to worship their Lorde God aryght . . . without your lowsie legerdemains, ye never were pleased."[10]

[7] G. Wickham, *Early English Stages*, I, 238f.

[8] *Pammachius*, 1538.

[9] For the political character of censorship (or toleration) in Tudor England, and its changes in direction and animus under successive sovereigns, see Siebert, *Freedom of the Press*, pp. 43-63; E. H. Miller, *Professional Writer*, Ch. vi, "Censorship"; P. Sheavyn, *Literary Profession*, pp. 39-63.

[10] Quotations from Chambers, *Elizabethan Stage*, I, 242 and n. On the use of the stage for different political purposes, see D. Beving-

As the legerdemain imputed to the Catholic party is exploded, toleration of plays is resumed. Under Elizabeth, the Privy Council is partial to the theatre. Under her Catholic predecessor Queen Mary, it attempts to put the theatre down. In 1553 the "playing of interludes . . . concerning doctrines in matters now in question and controversy" is prohibited. In 1557 "players and pipers strolling through the kingdom" are open to prosecution, as they enact "naughty plays." Within the city of London, no play is to be authorized, "except the same be first seen and allowed." Queen Mary approves the zeal of the Mayor of Canterbury, who reacts to the performance of a "profane" play in his city by silencing the players. But King Edward VI, whose sympathies are Protestant, is also concerned to promote "the inhibition of Players." He fears the Catholic bias of the interludes as making "towards sedition" (1549).

Clerical persons like Wylley and Bale defend their sort of theatre against the prohibition of anti-Catholic plays by the Crown.[11] Clerical persons a half century later, assuming collectively the name of Martin Marprelate, attack the theatre as an ally of the Established Church and Crown. It is not the form that is in question, or not at first, but the content. Elizabeth is not more inclined than King Edward to tolerate in interludes the "depraving or despising" of the Book of Common Prayer.[12] But plays are agreeable so long as they are circumspect: in moral terms, as they are free of "ribaudry" or "lesinge" (lying). This qualified approval is bestowed

---

ton, *Tudor Drama and Politics*, esp. Ch. i, "Some Approaches to Topical Meaning."
[11] 34 and 35 Henry VIII, *c.*1.   [12] 1559; I Elizabeth, *c.*2.

in an early treatise on the Ten Commandments (*Dives et Pauper*, c. 1410). It is often reaffirmed. When, in the last year of the reign of Henry VIII, Parliament takes order with the stage on its polemical side (1543), it does not question plays whose more equable business is "the rebuking and reproaching of vices and the setting foorth of vertue; so allways the saide songes, playes, or enterludes meddle not with the interpretacions of Scripture, contrarye to the doctrine set foorth . . . by the Kinges Majesty." The proviso is critical, and not simply as it touches Holy Writ.

Players are intolerable as they "gird at the greatest personages of all estates,"[13] or "cut the reputations throat of the more eminent rank of Cittizens with corroding scandals," or as they "strike at the head of Nobility, Authority, and high-seated Greatnesse."[14] Players who become involved in matters of state or cast "aspersions on men of eminent rank and quality . . . deserve no better censure, than as they whipt, so to bee whipt themselves for their labour: for they must know . . . that some things are priviledged from jest."[15] Furred robes and gowns are privileged. And hence it is not permitted to lay open "the faults and scandalls of great men, as Magistrates, Ministers, and such as hold publicke places,"[16] or to look askance at "Princes and Potentates."[17] Players and playwrights who think they "may pish in any mans face, intermeddle with the 2. edged sworde of the state." They are to understand that it is

---

[13] Epistle to *French Academy*, 1594 ed.
[14] *This World's Folly*, B3.   [15] *English Gentleman*, p. 192.
[16] *Vertues Common-wealth*, P3-v.
[17] Crashaw, *Virginia Sermon*, 1610, p. 63.

130

fit "for the authority of Princes and Governours of the commonwealth, every where to bee maintained in their royall state, without any manner of spot or touch of derogation." Failing this understanding, instruction in a harder truth awaits them. "It is not safe drawing out of Lions teeth."[18]

Contentiousness is reprehensible, as it means that men of position "are nickt and nipped, railed and reviled by these snarling curre-dogs" who are "our common Stage-players and Comicke-writers."[19] But contentiousness is acceptable and even commendable, so long as the poet is contentious for the right.

The Tudors, who patronize the secular theatre, undertake at the same time to destroy the medieval mysteries and moralities. This animus is, however, doctrinal; which means, paradoxically, it has to do with the supremacy of the secular state. A performance of the Creed play, which the York Corporation wishes to sponsor (1568), is frustrated by the Dean of York Minster, Matthew Hutton. The Dean is speaking, however, not in his character of clerical bigot but in his official role as a member of the Queen's Commission for Ecclesiastical Causes in the North. The formal reasons he adduces are mixed: he sees "many things that . . . [he] cannot allow because they be disagreeinge from the sincerity of the gospell." But it is the Erastian more than the Reformer who wonders "how the state will beare it," and who requires consequently that the play "shuld not be played."[20]

[18] Melton, *Sixe-Folde Politician*, pp. 30, 40f.
[19] Vaughan, *Spirit of Detraction*, p. 110.
[20] Wickham, I, 114f.

The rebellion of the Northern Lords (1569), as it is led by Roman Catholics, sharpens the prejudice against the old religious drama. The Archbishop of York, supported explicitly by the political power (as vested in the Lord President of the North), forbids religious plays at Chester (1571). Successive mayors of that city are summoned before the Privy Council for allowing, in defiance of the edict of Church and State, performances of the Chester cycle at Whitsun. The York Paternoster play is mounted just once more. Then the manuscript is seized and disappears forever (1572). Pleading "superstition and idolatry," Archbishop Grindal suppresses the mysteries at York and at Wakefield (1576) just as, a decade before, he had sought to drive the theatre from London. Grindal believes, with his colleague Dean Hutton, that "now . . . [is] the happy time of the gospell." But he identifies this happiness with a wider diffusion of the Puritan ethic: Work, for the night is coming! It is this unwavering bias that aligns him with the Privy Council against the ancient Catholicism of the North and, in a different context, with the London Corporation against the Crown.[21]

The Crown, in its bias, is also notably constant. Henry VII entertains four players of interludes in his household, and Prince Arthur, his own company (1498). That is true of the young Henry VIII (1506). As James ascends the throne, the protection of the players passes from the nobility: Shakespeare's company is known hereafter as the King's Men (1603).[22] The transferring of title carries with it explicit sanction to

[21] Wickham, I, 114f.; Craig, *English Religious Drama*, p. 360f.
[22] State Papers, 1614, p. 242; 1628, p. 333.

perform "within any towne halls, or Mouthalls, or other convenient places within the liberties, and freedome of any other Citty, University, Towne, or Borough whatsoever within our said Realmes and dominions." The King's subjects are willed and commanded "not only to permitt and suffer" the players, without let or molestation, "but also to be aiding and assisting to them if any wrong be to them offered."[23]

In the last years of Elizabeth, under the patronage of the Lord Chamberlain, this premier company performs at Court an average of three times a year; in the first decade of the new reign, performances more than quadruple. Elizabeth, who is not conspicuously openhanded, disburses annually to Shakespeare's fellows approximately 35 pounds (1594-1602); under James their average yield of 131 pounds (1603-1607) is supplemented by an allowance for the purchase of the royal livery it is their ambiguous privilege to wear.[24] As if he is intent on fulfilling the foolish character assigned him by a Whiggish posterity, James infuriates his Puritan subjects by making legal such amusements as dancing and archery and Whitsun Ales on the Sabbath.[25] Charles, who reissues his father's proclamation and in a less forgiving age, is more foolish and courageous. The City is admonished to permit the reopening of the London theatres, after a temporary closing (1604). In the teeth of clerical opposition, the King brings to Edinburgh a troupe of English actors and licenses their playing

[23] Discussion follows V. Gildersleeve, *Government Regulation of the Elizabethan Drama.*
[24] Bentley, *Shakespeare and His Theatre*, pp. 68f., 92.
[25] *Book of Sports*, 1618.

133

(1617). Subsequently he gives his sanction to a new theatre in Lincoln's Inn Fields (1620). The city English prove, however, more dour than the Scots; the royal sanction is withdrawn. It is a prelude to the ultimate capitulating of the Crown and the closing of all theatres a generation later.

These two events are associated in more than chronological ways. "O peerless poesie, where is then thy place?" asks Edmund Spenser in his October eclogue. Spenser, who anticipates his eviction from the "Prince's palace," which is the forging house of poetry, does not suppose that the "breast of baser birth" is likely to afford him entertainment. It is an accurate supposition.

The involvement of the Crown in the petty fortunes of poets and playwrights runs counter to expectation. "Of course, the fellow is a damned crank!" says King Edward VII, on attending a performance of *Arms and the Man*. But the support of the Crown for idle poetry does not depend on approbation of the thing itself. Art, like government and war and the sporting life and the priestly function, is by convention an aristocratic activity. It is the prerogative of a leisure class. To attack it is to menace the pretensions of that class. In covert ways, it is to menace the Crown itself.[26]

[26] For the role of the aristocrat as patron, and the poet as retainer, see Sheavyn, *Literary Profession*, pp. 8-20, 212-38; E. H. Miller, *Professional Writer*, pp. 96f., 105-110; and, in the Caroline period, D. Mathew, *Social Structure in Caroline England*, pp. 114-17. Samuel Daniel (quoted in Miller, p. 106), sees himself as dependent absolutely on Queen Elizabeth:

> I, who by that most blessed hand sustain'd,
> In quietnes, do eate the bread of rest;
> And by that all-reviving powre obtain'd
> That comfort which my Muse and me hath blest.

134

The patronage of princes fosters the art of miniature painting and permits it to attain to the level of excellence embodied in the work of Nicholas Hilliard or the brothers Limburg. Artists in search of a commission, like Isaac Oliver or John Souch or, on the Continent, Jan Van Eyck, apply for their substance to noblemen like the Duke of Berry or the Earl of Leicester, or to a royalist commander like Sir Thomas Aston[27] or a royalist politician like the Chancellor Nicholas Rolin. The man of baser birth, as he cannot indulge a taste for the exquisite, comes to look on this taste as pernicious. In his books, there are no illuminations.[28] It is required of him that he make "no graven Image . . . Nor picture be it greate or smalle."[29] His character is that of the plain and honest man, who wears no welt or guard. Like the country landlord in Greene's romantic comedy, he "cannot trick it up with poesies, / Nor paint . . . [his] passions with comparisons, / Nor tell a tale of Phoebus and his loves."[30] That is, however, not a source of dismay but satisfaction.

The painter or the poet or musician, as they see how the wind is blowing, take service with the gentleman, who is willing and able to keep them. "Neither do they want some Mecenas," says Henry Crosse, "to Patronize their witlesse workes . . . or recompence their idle labours."[31] If they are not themselves of gentle blood, they wear, by close contact with accumulated wealth

---

[27] Aston was painted by Souch in 1625.
[28] See discussion in J. Huizinga, *The Waning of the Middle Ages*, p. 261.
[29] *Court of Virtue*, Hvi.
[30] *Friar Bacon and Friar Bungay*, iii.iii.
[31] *Vertues Common-wealth*, O3-v.

or unbroken prerogative, the gentleman's colors. The finest music of the Renaissance is produced in the chapels of the courts: as by Dufay in Burgundy, or William Byrd in Westminster or Greenwich, or Heinrich Isaak in the Florence of Lorenzo, or Johannes Ockeghem in the household of the kings of France.[32] Victoria is attached as chaplain to the Spanish princess Maria, the sister of Philip II; and John Dunstable to the retinue of the Duke of Bedford, the brother of Henry V. Orlando Gibbons, two hundred years later, is chapel organist to Charles I. It is the Duke of Newcastle to whom the playwright Thomas Shadwell defers as "the only Maecenas of our Age." This opulent man, "while others detract from Poetry, or at least neglect it . . . not only encourages it by . . . [his] great Example, but protects it too"—by unclasping his purse.[33]

On his largesse, the player depends absolutely. The player is hateful for various reasons, but not least because he is a retainer. He wears the badge and the livery of the lord in whose household he serves. Players, says Martin Marprelate, who is not ordinarily given to ironic understatement, are "plaine rogues, save only for their liveries."[34] The player is exempted by royal edict from the sumptuary laws.[35] It is a privilege he enjoys from the fifteenth century forward. A statute of Henry VIII (1510) associates him in this particular with ecclesiastics and with functionaries at Court. The asso-

---

[32] Ockeghem, c.1425–c.1495, spent 40 years in the service of three French kings.
[33] Dedication to *Epsom Wells*, 1672.
[34] *Martin Junior's Epilogue*, ?1589, p. 330 in ed. Pierce, 1911.
[35] Under Henry IV, Edward IV, Henry VIII.

ciation is important symbolically, and also in material ways. Though Elizabeth endeavors to "sette down the limits of apparel to every degree," the players transcend these limits with impunity. Gosson has observed how "the very hyerlings of some of our players, who stand at the reversion of 6 s. by the week, jet under gentlemen's noses in suits of silke."[36] But the player has no difficulty in procuring the gentleman's indulgence. Like Anthony Munday, in his salad days a player as well as a writer, he abases himself before his aristocratic master as "*humilissimo, e Divotissimo, e sempre osservandissimo Vasallo e Servitore*."[37]

The detractor of stage plays perceives and enforces this connection. "To be accounted a noble mans jester is," in his opinion, "to be esteemed a mercinary Foole."[38] It is on the adjective that he places the heaviest stress. Assailing the "idle life" of players, who have attained nonetheless to "great abundance of wealth," he ventures to look higher, at the "unthrifts and profuse spenders" who are their noble patrons.[39] That is a significant and an ominous conjunction. Munday, the dismal draper, is concerned to deplore it in his more considered *Retrait from plaies and Theatres*. (Inconsistency does not trouble Anthony Munday.) Are plays "to be suffered and praised," he inquires, "because they please the rich, and content the Noble man, that always lives

---

[36] *School of Abuse*; quoted in Chambers, *Elizabethan Stage*, iv, 204.

[37] Dedication to *Mirrour of Mutabilitie*, 1579. The aristocratic master is Edward de Vere. For the servility of the poet before the patron, see Sheavyn, pp. 33-38; E. H. Miller, Ch. iv, "Patronage."

[38] I. G., *Refutation*, G3.   [39] D2-3, G2.

in ease?" The answer is emphatic and scornful: "not so.
A two legged Asse may be clothed in gold, a man of
honor may be corrupt of judgment." Mostly, however,
the attack on the patron is more circumspect than this.

Early in the sixteenth century, Henry Cornelius
Agrippa, an atrabiliar physician who is valiant for the
single truth, composes a philippic against the vanity of
art.[40] His animus is partly conventional: for example,
he denounces poetry as the father of lies. But partly he
is moved to write by his detestation of the hierarchy on
whose patronage the life of poetry depends. More is in-
volved, in Agrippa's attack on art, than the making of
an Erasmian paradox. The attack on art is a stalking-
horse. Sir John Harington makes this clear in the *Apolo-
gie of Poetrie* with which he introduces his translation
of Ariosto (1591). In Agrippa's censuring of the poets,
as Harington remarks very shrewdly, he "hath spared
neither miters nor scepters." Essentially he is taking
"his pleasure of greater matters then Poetry," as in
identifying the "courts of Princes," where poetry flour-
ishes, with "a Colledge . . . of Tyrants . . . [and] op-
pressors," and in affirming that "noble men and . . .
great officers of the common welth" are not so much
"the pillers of the state" as "robbers and peelers of the
realme."[41]

The poet participates in this indictment as he enacts
the role of Baucis, serving Jove in a wooden dish. That
is how Robert Greene presents himself to the Earl of
Cumberland, in dedicating his vulgar novel *Pandosto*
(1588). Munday is more fulsome, in coming forward as

[40] *De incertitudine et vanitate scientiarum et artium*, 1531.
[41] G. G. Smith, II, 200.

138

a poor herdsman who offers incense to Jupiter on pieces of broker potsherd.[42] But Jupiter is sometimes a poet himself: "even the greatest Monarches and Princes, as well Christian as Heathen, have exercised their Invention herein."[43] Puttenham, who believes that poets have been fortunate as they are "cunning Princepleasers,"[44] is supplied abundantly with illustrations: like John Skelton, who serves as tutor to Henry VIII; or William Cornish, in his function as Master to the Children of the Chapel Royal; or like the poet Chaucer, who is understood to flourish as he wins the favor of Richard II. "Poets in general," on the authority of one of their number, "have received such countenance and approbation from the most eminent'st Princes, as their Poems never wanted Patrons, nor the Authors themselves Benefactors." Henry IV is a happiness to John Gower, and Edward IV to John Hardyng. "And Henry the eighth, for a few Psalmes of David translated and turned into English Metre by Sternhold, made him groome of his Privy Chamber."[45] Boccaccio can call to mind "many instances of poets who enjoyed at their pleasure the friendship and domestic intercourse of kings and nobles, such as never fall to the lot of crude and oafish men."[46] Whatever the identity of the mysterious Mr. W. H. who figures in the dedication to Shakespeare's sonnets, it is clear that gentility describes him. He is not to be con-

[42] Dedication to Essex of Munday's romance, *Palladine of England*, 1588.
[43] Peacham, *Compleat Gentleman*, Ch. x.
[44] Bk. 1, Ch. viii.
[45] Brathwait, *English Gentleman*, pp. 189f.
[46] *Genealogy of the Pagan Gods*, xiv, xi; ed. Osgood (1930), 1956, p. 55.

fused with the supposititious printer and stationer William Hall, or the player Willy Hughes (Shakespeare imitating Oscar Wilde), or the inconsiderable playwright William Haughton. Neither is *Macbeth*, on the day of its premier performance, to be imagined as complimenting the livery masters and their journeymen at Leadenhall. That is an honor reserved for the King at Hampton Court.

The dramatist rejoices in the title of "Servant to His Majesty"; or he desires "less passionately . . . to be esteemed a poet than to be thought [the] most humble, most obedient, and most faithful servant" of the royal highness to whom he addresses his play.[47] But that is not in token of the native supremacy which belongs to the aristocrat. What is critical is the willingness of this well-endowed person to squander his resources in the public eye, as by lending "a ready hand to raise the dejected spirits of the contemned sons of the Muses."[48] The presumptive poet Thomas Hoccleve anticipates this liberal hand in the begging letters he circulates in quest of a titled supporter. Spenser, who composes adulatory sonnets in preface to the *Faerie Queene*, is hardly less barefaced; or that failed courtier "Mr. Aurelian Townshend, a poor and pocky poet," in endeavoring "to sell an hundred verses . . . at sixpence apiece, fifty shillings an hundred."

To the supplications of the poet, the merchant or the landed gentleman is largely indifferent. It does not follow that he is hostile to poetry, per se. Lionel Cran-

[47] Elkanah Settle, *Love's Revenge*, 1675; Sir George Etherege, *The Man of Mode*, 1676.
[48] Massinger, dedicating *The Renegado*, 1624.

140

field is discovered, on one occasion, taking pleasure in the company of John Donne.[49] The London Corporation, in its relentless attack on the stage, is not inspired perceptibly by esthetic or philosophic considerations. The poet is more attractive and less complex than his antagonist, in that he does what he does *con amore*. Samuel Daniel, in a noble passage from *Musophilus*, avows his contempt for the public neglect of his poems. It counts for nothing in the scale, against

> The love I beare unto this holy skill:
> This is the thing that I was borne to doo,
> This is my Scene, this part must I fulfill (ll. 576-78).

The critic who denounces poetry as he associates it with the college of tyrants and oppressors is not much concerned, at bottom, to argue questions of holiness or turpitude. He perceives that behind the stage, and the poet and playwright, stands the noble patron. It is this perception that sustains and exacerbates the long quarrel between the City and the Crown.

The development in the Middle Ages of the poetry known as *fin amor* is explicable partly as the pressing of an attack on the exclusivism of the feudal aristocracy. The lesser nobility who sponsor this attack are not much removed in time from their ancient status as *ministeriales* of the manor. Their success in transcending that status is attested, as they are knighted and enfeoffed with land. The same connection holds for their emulous counterparts in the England of Elizabeth and James. The dissenting clergyman John Northbrooke dedicates his tract against the stage to "his good friend" Sir John

[49] Tawney, *Business and Politics Under James I*, pp. 276f.

Young. This friend is not so imposing a figure as Sir Francis Walsingham, to whom Gosson dedicates *Playes Confuted*. But he also has aspired successfully to knighthood, and so he is not negligible either.

It does not signify, or not in this context, whether the detractor of plays and poetry believes, with Plato, that art is intrinsically vicious or, with Aristotle, that it is a purgation and so a good. Art is among the perquisites of great station. The interdicting of art, as in the polemics of Gosson and Munday and Henry Cornelius Agrippa, functions partly as the means to an end.

The end for which the new man is bidding is a more substantial place. The aristocrat comes between him and the achieving of this place. But he does not attack the aristocrat directly: that is not thinkable in the sixteenth and early seventeenth centuries. He seeks to pattern himself on the man whose place he covets, first of all by assuming the visible marks of beatitude. Ultimately, this attempt is unsuccessful. As its failure becomes apparent, the attack on hereditary privilege is pressed with increasing overtness. The tokens or accouterments of privilege are called in question. This is, on one side, the genesis of the war against poetry. Its entail is esthetic, and vastly political. The closing of the theatres is coincident with, or rather it betokens, a major shift in the understanding and evaluation of poetry. It betokens also the dispossessing of the privileged man. This is to say that the war against poetry recapitulates, like a metonymic figure, the passing of the old-fashioned or medieval psychology and the beginnings of the modern world. In terms of this figure, the process of transition, or supersession, is as follows.

As the seventeenth century opens, the new man endeavors to purchase the distinction which is not his by hereditary right.[50] But this firenew nobility he acquires is understood to be a brummagem thing. "Our new heraldry is hands, not hearts": Othello to Desdemona. The contempt for acquired distinction is intolerable and so of course it is absurd. "When Adam delved and Eve span, who was then the gentleman?" The troubadours and *trouvères*, as this sentiment occurs to them, express in their poetry the point of view of the class from which they derive. It differs sharply from that of the hereditary aristocracy, whose claim is made to blood. The new man, as he endeavors to wrest from the possessors of privilege the letters patent by which they possess it, looks elsewhere for the criterion of excellence. He finds this criterion not in lineage but in prowess or in courtesy.

Prowess is invoked when, in the fifteenth century, the kings of Spain undertake to put down the ancient nobility of Castile. "Since the hope of guerdon is the spur to just and honorable actions"—I am quoting from a statute enacted at Toledo in the reign of Ferdinand and Isabella—"when men perceive that offices of trust are not to descend by inheritance, but to be conferred on merit, they will strive to excel in virtue, that they may attain its reward."[51] It is of this more tangible virtue that the troubadour, shut away from the recognition he desires, makes his luxuriant song. "Know that . . . [nobility] comes not from the womb . . . Did they issue

[50] For the purchase of titles under James I, see Stone, "Elizabethan Aristocracy," p. 41.
[51] W. H. Prescott, *Ferdinand and Isabella*, 1856, I, 200.

from it on Horseback?"[52] Nobility is identified with performance. It is signalized by the gentle heart.[53]

That is a revolutionary proposal. It is also a familiar *topos*, at least from the time of Juvenal, and recurrent in the Middle Ages and in the humanistic disputations of the Renaissance. But in the latter period, the vitality of this ancient idea is dramatically renewed. To Henry Medwall, composing the first secular drama in English, the appeal to merit is not merely a theme for academic debate. Henry VIII implies its new and more vigorous content, in preferring "the meanest man . . . to rule and govern . . . without respect of the very estate of the personage."[54]

This waiving of respect for inherited status is heady doctrine, and vastly consequential for the future. But it is not much entertained in the beginning by the man of baser birth, who supports the whimsical business carried on by his betters in the rarefied air at the top. In the beginning, he has recourse to emulation. He melts down his lands against the purchase of flame-colored stockings, or he cultivates elegance with such assiduity as not

[52] *Le Roman de Fauvel.* Discussion draws on M. Valency, *In Praise of Love*, 1958.

[53] Thus the burden of the famous canzone, *Al cor gentil*, with which Guido Guinizelli initiated the "sweet new style" in thirteenth-century Italy.

[54] See Medwall, *Fulgens and Lucrece* (1497); and Bevington, *Tudor Drama and Politics*, pp. 44f., 86f. Fromm, *Escape from Freedom*, p. 59, comments (after Tawney) on the new primacy in the Renaissance of the gentle heart as against the claims of lineage: "The individual was left alone; everything depended on his own effort, not on the security of his traditional status."

to make water unless in a cinquepace. The sumptuary laws beget in him a contempt that is almost aristocratic. "By the Lord," exclaims Hamlet, who takes note of all things, "the age is grown so picked that the toe of the peasant comes so near the heel of the courtier, he galls his kibe." Like Shakespeare's petty hero, Alexander Iden, who kneels a poor squire and rises up a knight, he buckles on the greaves and cushes (*2Henry VI*). Like the expectant Dapper in Jonson's comedy, he consorts with the small poets of the time; or, like Kastril the country gentleman, he comes up to town to learn "to carry quarrels, as gallants do; to manage 'em by line."

This imitative zeal is affecting and not wholly unproductive. In the last resort, however, it is not the brutishness of Ajax or the lechery of Paris which constitutes their particular excellence. "The reward of preferment," says Dante, "goes to the noble as naturally as an effect follows from its cause."[55] Dante, who is aware of the compulsive ardor of Aeneas, esteems him more highly for the royal blood in his veins. Honor is not an effect but a cause.

Emulation fails. The common man, as he seeks to pattern himself on his aristocratic master, discovers that virtue is a birthright. This otiose proposition is illustrated vividly in the conduct of martial business. War, says Mark Antony, is "the royal occupation!" Here also, the aspiration of the common man is unavailing. Prowess in arms is reserved to his betters, as also the status that requites it. The common man retains the privilege of shedding his blood. Only he may not shed it with élan.

[55] *Monarchia*, Bk. ii, Ch. iii.

145

On this point, contemporary poets and playwrights are emphatic. The noble Pyrocles, in Sidney's *Arcadia*, is incensed by the boorish Dametas; but "the baseness of the villain yet made me stay my hand." In this case, the villain may thank his stars. He is not always so lucky. Shakespeare's histories offer corroboration. The formal combat between Horner the Armorer and Peter, his man, is not intrinsically a laughing matter. The apprentice strikes his master to the ground; the master dies. Nonetheless, the action is comic, by design. The contestants oppose each other not with the lance and sword but with staves to which a sandbag is fastened (*2Henry VI*). The black-letter lawbooks, prescribing the etiquette of trial by battle, admit in such a contest only these rustical weapons, "inasmuch as villeins have no honor." The French soldiers who decline to do battle with the knightly Talbot forfeit their honor. As they do not take up their arms like true gentlemen, they are known for muleteers and peasant footboys (*1Henry VI*). The footboy or villein may follow his master into the breach. But he hangs about the field of battle by courtesy of the noble persons who contend there. "What prisoners of good sort are taken?" asks King Henry after Agincourt. The English Herald, telling over the resonant names, concludes, as if an afterthought has struck him: "besides common men." Their function is to fill a pit. "Chaff and bran! porridge after meat!" That is how Pandarus, in *Troilus and Cressida*, describes them. War "is a schoole where all the principles tending to honour, are taught if truly followed" (Massinger, *A New Way to Pay Old Debts*). These principles are

146

lost, however, on the "vulgar sort, whose judgment is so corrupt and crooked, that they cannot discerne what true honor and dignity is."[56]

The appeal to judgment is partly a red herring. The man of noble lineage, says Ben Jonson satirically, is "descended in a rope of titles," from Guy of Warwick or Bevis of Hampton or King Arthur—"or from whom the Herald will." His blood "is now become past any need of virtue."[57] To the annalist of courtesy, like Henry Peacham the Younger in his *Compleat Gentleman*, it is blood that distinguishes the "intruding upstart, shot up with the last nights Mushroome, from an ancient descended & deserved Gentleman, whose Grandsires have had their shares in every foughten field by the English since Edward the first."[58]

This insistence on distinction is not confined to the practice of arms. Neither is it peculiar to the ancient descended gentleman. In an age of privilege like the Renaissance, the practice of all the arts, those that are useful as well as liberal, is itself a privilege. Each craft approximates an independent enclave. Society is made to cohere by the operation of organic filaments: that is the nostalgic view of the Victorians after the old relation between classes and kinds of men has dissolved. But society is also fragmented by the segregating of its individual members into groups. Each of these groups—whether organized in terms of productive function or

[56] Lodowick Bryskett, *A Discourse of Civill Life*, 1606, p. 191; C. Watson, *Shakespeare and the Renaissance Concept of Honor*, p. 91.

[57] Underwood xliv, "A speach according to Horace."

[58] Ed. Gordon, pp. 160f.

specific expertise, as the guilds and the livery companies are organized, or along the invisible but still sharply definitive lines of blood and class—declares its particularity. Abhorson the hangman, in *Measure for Measure*, demurs at the assistance of Pompey the bawd, as he is not enrolled in the mystery which is the craft. This distaste the hangman evinces is a matter of corporate pride. The leather-worker or the goldsmith or farrier—Pompey would say, even the bawd—is dedicated not simply to self-interest but to fulfilling the distinctive standards of his craft. It is, of course, a happiness when these two coincide, as in the hopeful observation of an Italian letter-writer that "the early riser makes a good profit, and can lie down at night in an inn."[59]

The ideal of the early riser is to drive up the standard of living as high as earning capacity allows. The effect on the serious activities of men is, therefore, to direct them with great singleness of purpose to the largest possible acquisition of wealth. It is also to discountenance labor that brings no pecuniary gain. The effect on consumption is to concentrate it along the lines which are most patent to those observers whose favorable opinion is sought. When Chaucer the pilgrim concludes his description of the really substantial persons who undertake the journey to Canterbury, he turns to the members of his own class. At once his tone changes. Now his eye is on the visible signs of material well-being or whatever tells against it. Appearance is everything, a fact which the narrator satirizes and also esteems.

[59] Niccolo dell'Ammannato, quoted in I. Origo, *Merchant of Prato*, p. xiii.

148

The aristocratic ideal is indifferent to the making of invidious comparisons in terms of pecuniary success. It puts a premium on the non-productive consumption of time. The goal of labor, as the aristocrat conceives it, is not to buy cheap, to make swiftly, and sell dear. It is to fashion, however slowly, an excellent thing, which is valued inversely to use. The gentleman who deigns to write poetry or plays must first acquit himself of the stigma of professionalism. His pose is that of the gifted but indifferent amateur. Politically and socially, he is inclined to adhere to an old-fashioned or conservative point of view. Money is beneath his notice. He does not compose, except for amusement. If what he composes is perfect, it is also a toy. The printer, who sees his polite effusions through the press, has no warrant from him. On the contrary: he does what he can to inhibit publication. That, at least, is his story.[60]

The larcenous or vulgar activity of the printer is contingent on his need to make a living. The gentleman is free of this constraint. His superiority follows. "The wisdom of a learned man cometh by opportunity of leisure" (Ecclesiasticus 37:24). That is how the aristocrat admonishes Poor Richard. He himself is not committed to a life of gainful employment. The peculiar fragrance

[60] E. H. Miller, Ch. i, "Authors in Their Milieu," and P. Sheavyn, pp. 165-69, describe the gentleman's disdain for professionalism, and his insistence on his own gentility and amateur status. For the connection among writers of conservatism and the amateur point of view, as also the professed contempt for financial reward, see Miller, pp. 23-26. The general devaluing of poetry as toys or trifles is documented by Miller, Ch. iii, "The Taste of the Audience," and Sheavyn, pp. 162-64. Miller (Ch. v, "Writers and Stationers") and Sheavyn (pp. 77-82) each discuss the supposed purloining of the gentleman's MS by pirate printers.

by which he is distinguished derives not from what he does but from what he fails to do. "Nobility taketh not his beginning, so much from abandoning of vice, as from giving over of base practise and mechanicall artes."[61] The aristocrat identifies base practice with the life of trade. He dedicates his own life to physical pleasure; very occasionally, to mental exercise also. This deifying of leisure as the basis of repute tends necessarily to limit production. Yet it is on increasing production that the standard of living for the many depends. This inhibition may be combated, as in Periclean Athens or in the ante bellum South, by the use of slave labor, working under a compulsion far more rigorous than that of reputability. Failing the existence of a chattel class, the plight of the many, whose freedom carries with it no privilege, grows acute. The road to the poorhouse runs through the college of tyrants and oppressors.

When privilege does not beckon, the outcry of the many against the few is not much heard. The more miserable, the less clamant. "Hunger is not ambitious." Stolypin, on the other hand, marshals the way to Lenin. The Tudors, as they help to give birth to an England in which the ambitious and industrious parvenu can make his way, give birth to the Commonwealth also.

Aristocratic leisure is the bane of the industrious man. But this leisured existence does not connote simple indolence or sloth. The aristocrat does not spend every hour in view of the multitude who are to be impressed with the spectacle of honorific idleness which, in the ideal scheme, makes up his life. The nodding plumes

[61] *Courtier's Academie*, p. 199.

which betoken the warlike hero belong to him by heredi-
tary right; so do the singing robes which betoken the
poet. These characteristic ornaments, which signify the
proper business of the privileged man, are united in the
person of Sir Philip Sidney, whom Spenser eulogizes
as "the most noble and virtuous gentleman most worthy
of all titles both of learning and chivalry."[62] This praise
is overmatched in the event. The life of Sidney is ad-
dressed to service (noblesse oblige), heroic ardor (as on
the fatal field of Zutphen), romantic and unrequited
love (that of the stargazer for the everchangeable star).
His hallmarks are breeding and elegance and wit. These
are conspicuous in the courtly verses he writes, or in the
sugared sonnets of his only begetting, which are handed
up to him by an untitled and impecunious poet. Sidney
receives almost forty dedications.[63] His favor is solicited
even by the poet-hater Gosson, who is alert to the use-
fulness of hedging his bets.

To emulate such a hero is not open to Everyman.
Partly, that is the idea. "Worldly want," says Count
Romei, "is the mother of Arts moechanicall, & wealth
of Artes liberall, and of noble and vertuous actions." But
these estimable actions "rather accompany the rich, then
poore, in that hee cannot have leasure, that wanteth
commings in."[64] In this way it happens that art becomes
the concern as well as the ensign of the best (or privi-
leged) man.

The ruinous prodigality by which the man of privi-
lege is recognized is manifest in his alacrity to do battle

[62] Dedication to *Shepherd's Calendar.*
[63] See F. B. Williams, Jr., *Index of Dedications.*
[64] *Courtier's Academie,* pp. 93, 249.

151

for an eggshell, or in the wearing of gorgeous apparel, or the lavish appointing of churches, or the engaging of hangers-on and retainers like the hundred knights and squires whom King Lear keeps at point.[65] It is manifest also in a negligent cultivating of the arts. The gentleman parades on the Field of the Cloth of Gold. Like Alençon or Essex, he participates in grand amours, or in a cabal to let loose the blood-dimmed tide of civil war. The "Illustrious Order of Mendicants" to which the gentleman belongs—the phrase is J. E. Neale's—is by no means an impecunious order.[66] The privilege of the gentleman carries with it enormous prestige—a word which means, in the root sense, deception or cozenage. The Earl of Leicester is a notable cozener. His indebtedness and that of his extravagant nephew, "our Sidney and our perfect man," approaches in modern currency to half a million pounds.[67] King Edward VI dispenses in annual payment a tenth of that sum to the secular musicians who entertain him.[68] When the Jacobean letter-writer John Chamberlain records the marriage of the Prince Palatine to Elizabeth, the daughter of King James (February 14, 1613), he attends in particular to

[65] Stone, "Anatomy of the Elizabethan Aristocracy," pp. 3-13, 21-5, describes an aristocracy living hopelessly beyond its means, and documents the conspicuous waste by which it is recognized—in clothing, hospitality, building of houses, sumptuous living in London, expenditure on jewelry, sports, retinues, the grand tour, dowries, and funerals, indebtedness to money lenders.

[66] Neale is quoted in E. H. Miller, p. 105. And compare Stone, "Elizabethan Aristocracy," p. 40, on the increase in corruption under James I "that at last made the tenure of responsible position a source of profit."

[67] Tawney's Wilson, pp. 32f.

[68] J. Stevens, *Music and Poetry in the Early Tudor Court*, p. 299.

a gown of the Lady Wotten's "that cost fifty pound a yard the embrodering."[69] But what delights the noble Englishman "beyond measure . . . [is] a very great retinue":[70] like the 1,000 servants in livery who accompany the Earl of Pembroke, or the 80 gentlemen in gold chains and Reading tawny whom Stowe assigns to the Earl of Oxford.[71]

The attendance which the gentleman dances is recompensed without relation to the utility of the service he performs. It is his crib and not the merchant's that stands at the King's mess. He holds a monopoly over high office, which is the source of his considerable fortune. Parliament is his private fief. If this gentleman is involved in litigation, the posting of a bond is waived. His unsupported word negates the sworn testimony of the common man. That is an important concession. Like Sidney, who announces to an inoffensive retainer that "I will thruste my Dagger into yow," the gentleman is very subject to spleen.[72] The ferocity which describes him goes unpunished, however; it is even a source of honor. France in the sixteenth century is a field of honor. Henri IV commutes the sentences of 7,000 duellists (1589-1610).[73] In fifteenth-century Castile, the *ricos hombres* or higher nobility, as their lives are busied with war "or with those martial exercises which reflect the image of it" (Prescott), are exempted from general taxation and imprisonment for debt. The personal alter-

[69] Chamberlain adds: "But this extreme cost and riches makes us all poor": Letter to Mrs. Carleton, *Letters*, ed. N. McClure, I, 226.

[70] *Italian Relation* (Report to the Venetian Senate), *c.*1503.

[71] C. Watson, p. 86; Stowe's *Survey*, 1618, p. 139.

[72] Ed. Feuillerat, p. 225.   [73] C. Watson, pp. 97, 70.

cation in which they engage convulses the kingdom. But it is a noble altercation, and therefore it is privileged. In Aragon, the right of the gentleman to appeal to arms is recognized by statute.[74] In Germany, the *Raubritter* or titled bravo, availing himself of this recognition, holds the countryside to ransom. It is not open to his subjects to remonstrate—or not yet.

The gentleman is practiced in the squandering of time and money and in the managing of *Fehden* or private quarrels; he is not otherwise remarkable. Like the wild Thracian in the Histories of Herodotus, he despises toil as beneath him and glories in deriving his income from plunder. It appears to him that "mechanicall, mercenary, or husbandmen . . . [are] unapt to vertue" —even those, in the engaging phrase of Count Romei, who are "borne of mechanicall parents."[75] Education is hateful to him, as to the aristocratic matron in the play by Oscar Wilde: "It puts one almost on a level with the commercial classes."[76] Mostly, he keeps the wind between this class and his nobility. In sixteenth-century France, says the traveler Fynes Moryson, "the Nobility scornes to be Marchants, thincking such traffique ignoble, according to the Heraults rules."[77] To live like a nobleman, as these rules are taken to heart, means ideally "to

[74] Prescott, I, lix-lxiii, xc.
[75] *Courtier's Academie*, pp. 249, 186.
[76] "Gentlemen's sons ought to be able to blow their horn skilfully, to hunt well, and to carry and train a hawk elegantly; but the study of letters is to be left to the sons of peasants": Richard Pace in E. H. Miller, *Professional Writer*, p. 40. And see Miller, Ch. vii, on the gentleman's scorn for learning.
[77] Quoted in C. Watson, p. 87.

live without doing anything" (Henri Pirenne).[78] "Why
are we rich, or great," Ben Jonson inquires ironically,

> except to show
> All license in our lives? What need we know
> More than to praise a Dog? or Horse? or speake
> The Hawking language? or our Day to breake
> With Citizens? let Clownes, and Tradesmen breed
> Their Sonnes to study Arts, the Lawes, the Creed:
> We will beleeve, like men of our owne Ranke,
> In so much land a yeare.[79]

This vacuous existence has the sanction of the religious
establishment which, as it supplies an ethos to the hier-
archical state, prepares its own mortification. The Son
of Sirach would like to know how that man can "get wis-
dom that holdeth the plough, and that glorieth in the
goad; that driveth oxen; and is occupied in their la-
bours; and whose talk is of bullocks" (Ecclesiasticus
38:25). It is a contemptuous question and implicit in it
is a stigmatizing of "the life of mechanicall artificers"
as "base, degenerating from vertue, and unworthy a
civill man."[80] Castiglione, who thinks that "in wars the
true provocation is glory," asserts that whoever takes
up arms "for lucres sake ... deserveth not the name of a
gentleman, but is a most vile merchant."[81]

Only the man of inherited means is the good man.
That is the old idea, and it is not very widely queried
until the Renaissance. In the received opinion of Aris-
totle, the citizen "must not lead a mechanic or a mercan-

[78] *History of Europe*, I, 142.
[79] Underwood, XLIV.   [80] *Courtier's Academie*, p. 195.
[81] *The Courtier*, Bk. 1; C. Watson, p. 88.

tile life, for such a life is ignoble and inimical to virtue."[82] Imperial Rome endorses this ancient superstition. The poor ploughman is likened to the ox that cuts the furrow; the senator, who is ipso facto a patrician, is enjoined from taking part in trade. The medieval chivalry, as it is indifferent to the idea of productive labor and profit, does not suppose that the merchant can find favor in the sight of God. *Homo mercator numquam aut vix potest Deo placere*: it is easier for a camel to thread the postern of a small needle's eye. That is how the medieval ecclesiastic is apt to respond to the aspirations of the mercantile class.[83]

Lucre, as it is earned, soils whatever it touches. "Base tike," says Ancient Pistol, "call'st thou me host? Now, by this hand, I swear I scorn the term." But lucre is indispensable. Nobility is wedded to the exercise of the liberal arts: "and because these cannot be freely exercised without riches, therefore are Riches necessary for the preservation of Nobility."[84] And so the vicious circle is closed. The breaking of the circle is the ingenious business of the seventeenth century. In the forwarding of this business, the attack on plays and poems is instrumental.

[82] *Politics*, Bk. VII, 8.   [83] Pirenne, I, 192.
[84] *Courtier's Academie*, p. 199.

VII The Tie That Binds

THE PRIVILEGED role which the gentleman claims for himself is agreeable to the caryatides who support it only so long as their bread and butter is not at issue. "God save Queen Elizabeth!" cries the Puritan lawyer John Stubbs, waving his hat with one hand as the Queen's executioner severs the other with a cleaver. Allegiance lapses, however, as his pockets are picked. Already in the thirteenth century the withholding of allegiance is suggested when a Castilian king is urged by his subjects to "bring his appetite within a more reasonable compass."[1] It is economic man who frames the hypothesis of a college of tyrants and oppressors. He discovers that special privilege is an ancient imposition, as it makes against his well-being. The glass of fashion is cracked, or it is a concave glass. "The pig, or the great, or the mighty, or the huge, or the magnanimous, are all one reckonings, save the phrase is a little variations."[2] It is apparent to Bishop Sprat that "Trafic, and Commerce have given mankind a higher degree than any title of Nobility."[3] The mercantile class, although it is denied the honorific occupations of the nobility, embraces, in the words of an ardent panegyrist, "the greatest propor-

[1] W. Lewis, *The Lion and the Fox*, n.d., p. 128.
[2] Fluellen in *Henry V*, iv, vii.
[3] *History of the Royal Society*, 1667; ed. Cope and Jones, p. 408.

157

tion of the intelligence, industry, and wealth of the state. In it are the heads that invent, and the hands that execute; the enterprise that projects, and the capital by which these projects are carried into operation" (Francis Place).[4]

The industrious man, who does not stand on an island of inherited wealth, is able to accomplish the excellent thing only through productive efficiency and thrift. But the excellence of what he does is not approved by the canons of reputability. And so he calls them in question.[5] "Whosoever will not labor, let him not eat": Hugh Latimer after St. Paul.[6] Against the venerable shibboleths of the privileged class, he invokes the wisdom of the present, which visits contempt on intangible production. This contempt finds an echo in popular speech. It used to be, says Tom Nashe, that when a man had "cosend or gone beyonde us," we would say of him that "hee hath playde the Merchant with us." Now, as the merchant attains his majority, the cozener is defined as one who plays the gentleman.[7] This gentleman is odious as the work in which he is supposed to participate brings no pecuniary return. The governing principle is that expressed in a trenchant phrase by Jonson in the *Poetas-*

[4] Quoted by E. Halevy from *Westminster Review*, Vol. I, Art. iv, in *History of Philosophic Radicalism* (1901-04), 1955, p. 286.

[5] As against the Thomistic and Aristotelian contempt for labor, sixteenth-century Protestantism decides that labor with the hands is good. Mental and manual toil are equated in dignity. See C. and K. George, *Protestant Mind*, pp. 131-33, and esp. p. 143: "To the Protestant, the most obviously godly calling is the most obviously economic or productive one: that of the husbandman, the artisan, the tradesman. We have here a genuine transvaluation of values."

[6] Quoted in L. B. Wright, *Middle Class Culture*, p. 173.

[7] *Christ's Tears over Jerusalem*, quoted in E. H. Miller, p. 193.

ter: "He, that hath coine, hath all perfection else." The aristocrat and his lady are perfect, as they emulate the peacock in dress. The industrious man earns his bread in the sweat of his face, and so he dresses plainly. It is natural that he collaborate in the elimination of that considerable area of human experience which is the province of poetry. Unlike the poet, who is concerned on his official side with the beautiful, the good, and the true, his principal concern is with pecuniary fitness. But as he achieves a more favored position, he does not defenestrate Poor Richard, as Poor Richard deserves. He continues to pay homage to the obsolete ideals of the early risers whose ranks he has quitted. From the eighteenth century forward, the drab costume of the worker denotes the respectable man. On this man, and whatever his income, honor enforces the choice of a profession. To the question: "Must every man, even gallant and great ones, have a calling?" the preacher answers affirmatively. He adds: "They that have none, or having any will not labour in it, are not worthy to eate."[8] But the writing of plays and poetry is not among the acceptable professions. Even so late as the eighteenth century, it remains a tenet of faith that "the Infidelity and Looseness of the Age is very much owing to the Play-Houses."[9] An associate of Jeremy Collier's persists in bringing forward "almost Two Thousand Instances" which illustrate the natural tendency of the stage "to Destroy Religion, and Introduce a General

[8] Hill, *Pathway*, R8.

[9] Anon., *A Representation of the Impiety and Immorality of the Stage*, 1704, p. 19. Anthony, *Collier Stage Controversy*, ascribes to Collier, pp. 10f.

159

Corruption of Manners."[10] "I tell you," says William Law, still laboring the point in the reign of George I, if "you go to hear a Play . . . you go to hear Ribaldry and Prophaneness."[11] The drama "is not meerly an unprofitable consumption of time, it is further improper," says President Witherspoon of Princeton, in the second half of the eighteenth century, "because it agitates the passions too violently, and interests too deeply, so as, in some cases, to bring people into a real, while they behold an imaginary distress."[12] Phylogenetic memories are strong.

The visible signs of beatitude are not reconstituted in every particular, as the present displaces the past. Continuity is more remarkable than change when, in the nineteenth century, Ruskin enumerates the activities of the playing class in his own time.[13] To the conventional repertory, Ruskin adds, however, the fooling about with money for its own sake. The conceding of dignity to this ultimate sport—"playing at counters," Ruskin calls it— is deeply significant for the great quarrel between the City and the Throne.

In the sixteenth and early seventeenth centuries, Jove on the throne is not open to censure. The dissenting minister is not satiric but prudential and in his myopic way sincere, in dedicating to King Charles a violent attack on the religious establishment, and hence on the

[10] Arthur Bedford, *Tracts*, 1706, 1719. Bedford's contribution to the Collier controversy is recapitulated in Anthony, Chs. xi-xiii.
[11] Law, *The Absolute Unlawfulness of the Stage-Entertainment*, 1726; Anthony, Ch. xiii.
[12] John Witherspoon, *A Serious Enquiry into the Nature & Effects of the Stage*, 1762.
[13] Introductory lecture to the *Crown of Wild Olive*.

monarchy as well (Henry Burton, *For God, and the King*, 1636). It is the business of a later and more forthputting age, "by writing, to persuade / That kings were useless, and a clog to trade" (*Absalom and Achitophel*, ll. 614f.). In the interim, censure is inferential and is visited at a remove: for example, by the heaping of obloquy on the poet and playwright. As the supremacy of the gentleman grows more onerous to those on whose shoulders he is sitting, whatever betokens it comes to seem abhorrent. Mostly, this abhorrence is assigned to the Puritan. But that is not tenable, or it is misleading. In the private chapel of the Earl of Essex, Puritan preachers receive a cordial welcome, as they suggest religious reasons for deposing the sovereign, "providing the cause were just."[14] Catholics are noticed also resorting to Essex House. Essex himself is neither Puritan nor Catholic. He is a disaffected man, and so he finds these allies congenial. That is the point his accusers urge against him when, subsequently, he is brought to trial: "As Catiline entertained the most seditious persons about all Rome to join with him in his conspiracy, so the Earl of Essex entertained none but papists, recusants and atheists for his abettors in this his capital rebellion against the whole estate of England."[15]

The condemnation of plays and poems is, on one side, a more circumspect version of this rebellion against the whole estate. It is not exclusively a Puritan phenomenon. The Puritan is, however, a conspicuous figure in the attack on the stage as he is hostile to the authority

[14] Two Sunday sermons preached in the Christmas season, 1600; Bowen, *Lion and the Throne*, p. 131.
[15] Sir Henry Yelverton; Bowen, p. 144.

that sustains it. Popular iconography tends not to notice this self-interested hostility, in presenting the Puritan as a type of the dyspeptic man,

> That in his censure each alike gainsayes,
> Poets in Pulpits, Holy Writ in Playes . . .
> That doth the selfe-accusing Oath refuse:
> That hates the Ale-house, and a Stage, and Stews.[16]

Sir Thomas Overbury's character of a Puritan is more suggestive, as it communicates his fundamental bias: "Anything that the law allows, but marriage and March beer, he murmurs at; what it disallows and holds dangerous, makes him a discipline."[17] Two centuries after this discipline is promulgated, the legislature of the state of Pennsylvania entertains a proposal to subsidize the stage (1785). The proposal fails of endorsement, but not from dyspepsia. On the affirmative side is the party of privilege. That is enough to arouse the enmity of the middle class.[18] Evidently, the play itself is not the thing.

Stephen Gosson, who is very fierce in condemning the theatre, is not a Puritan, and in fact assails the continental reformers as "Vermine." William Crashaw in his sermons calumniates the Puritan as well as the player. Robert Anton, the poeticizing antagonist of stage plays, writes his book to controvert the errors of Amsterdam.[19] Bishop Wilkins denies the validity of poetic language (as by contriving a Real Character), and ministers as

---

[16] "The Description of a Puritan" appended to "A Dialogue . . . by . . . Dr. Martin Mar-prelat" [1589].

[17] Quoted in C. Cullen, *Puritanism and the Stage*, p. 180.

[18] C. and M. Beard, *The Rise of American Civilization*, 1, 466.

[19] Dedication to *Vices Anotimie*.

chaplain to the Prince Elector Palatine (who is a patron of poets). Sir Thomas Lucy, who is supposed to have harried the young Shakespeare, is able to reconcile his Puritan leanings with financial support of the stage. The same is true of the Earl of Leicester. Sidney's friend Justus Lipsius, professor of theology at Leyden, loves profane learning so well, and is so confident in that learning, as to recite on demand random quotations from Tacitus with a dagger against his bare chest. At Christ's College, Cambridge, the Puritan divine Richard Bernard edits and translates the comedies of Terence (1598). Terence is a popular playwright, but dead a long time. In the same decade, the Cambridge Council suggests to the Vice Chancellor of the University the wisdom of excluding all "playes, or enterludes of common players" (1593).[20] It is the privileged position these players enjoy at which the thrust is aimed.

The man of the new dispensation is inclined to speak bitterly of the poet and playwright as he identifies them with the party of privilege. The language he uses is the denunciatory language of the Old Testament. It is "a fountain filled with blood, drawn from Immanuel's veins." His appeal to outraged morality is genuine, but it is not the whole story. In his attack on the vanity of art is comprehended an oblique attack on the statecraft of the Tudors and Stuarts, and the polity of Hooker and Laud. That is why the Crown is partial to the poet and playwright. A modern historian of letters, assessing Jeremy Collier's attack on the stage in the closing years of the seventeenth century, describes it as "equivalent

[20] Thompson, *Controversy*, pp. 93f.

to his hurling a dart at the profligacy of the Stuart dynasty."[21] I would omit the adverbial phrase.

King James speaks explicitly to the vital connection of Church and State in prophesying to Robert Cecil that "when soever the ecclesiastical dignity . . . shall be turned into contempt and vanish in this kingdom, the kings hereof shall not longer prosper in their government and the monarchy shall fall to ruin."[22] The intimate involvement of art in this connection is vivid to revolutionaries like the Puritan divine Henry Burton. Art, as Burton sees it, is an appanage of Church and State. In a pair of sermons against the bishops and their supposed allegiance to Rome, he proceeds sequentially to an indictment of the stage. That is as he identifies each with a common master. "Court Gnathoes" or parasites have usurped the direction of the Church. And they are not "content, to abuse our pious Princes eares in the Pulpit, but also on the Stage." Episcopacy, in the lexicon of the anti-episcopalian, "is a scurilous Enterlude."[23] The definition is striking, as it suggests the oneness of the prelate and player. And now the codicil, in which the wisdom of King James is approved: as wicked rulers and their satellites seek to "devoure Christs Vineyard, while they Suppresse the Preaching of the Word," so "the Ninivites shall rise in judgment against this generation."[24] What the dissenter is proclaiming, and men-

[21] Anthony, *Collier Stage Controversy*, p. 26.

[22] Quoted in Bowen, pp. 299f.

[23] *For God, and the King*, pp. 47f.

[24] P. 149. For the casual association of bishops with stage players in the popular mind, see More's *Richard III*, ed. Yale, 1963, ii. 79/27–81/10. For the connection of theatre and church, see Barish, "Exhibitionism and the Anti-Theatrical Prejudice," pp. 6-8, 13.

acing under the guise of a figure, is a triple association of the artist, the orthodox churchman, and the Crown.

The new philosopher or the entrepreneur do not indulge so exotic a vocabulary as the religious enthusiast. This difference between them is, however, superficial. In the attack on the poet and playwright, each is impelled at bottom by a similar psychology, each speaks from the same point of view. The tie that binds is a common dedication to naked truth, divested of adornment and recognized and acknowledged as it bears.

The association of the poet with the established order, in which this comelier and more useful truth is occluded, is evidently attested by concurrent events. Burton loses his ears in the pillory (1636); King Charles, at Oxford, attends a tragicomedy by the dramatist William Strode in which the Puritan is ranged against the prince and the poet (*The Floating Island*, 1636); Archbishop Laud, who is Burton's most conspicuous target, bestows his patronage on the dramatist William Cartwright, who is also required to entertain the King, in the year of Burton's degradation (*The Royal Slave*, 1636).

Only a little later, Parliament has become sufficiently powerful—it is the time of Pym's ascendancy—to attack the bishops in a petition addressed directly to the King. Episcopacy, as the petitioners define it, is a compound of "manifold evils." These include, on the one hand, "the great increase of idle, lewd and dissolute, ignorant and erroneous men in the ministry" and, on the other, "the swarming of lascivious, idle, and unprofitable books and pamphlets, playbooks and ballads."[25] In

[25] Petition of Dec. 11, 1641; C. Friedrich, *The Age of the Baroque*, p. 289.

the conjunction, metonymy governs. The bishop is presented in the poet and playwright.

The conjunction has been verified a half century before. To distinguish among "these stage-players, these prelates, these popes, these devils" seems to Martin Marprelate a splitting of hairs. Identity of interest yokes them together. The bishops, in their usurpation of temporal authority, are abetted—very logically, Martin thinks—by "rimers and stage players (that is, plaine rogues)." As they are aware of the source of their livelihood, they "do the bidding of the Canterbury Caiphas, with the rest of his AntiChristian beasts."[26] The player, who has "not so much as an honest calling to live in the commonwealth," finds his proper calling in trimming up "the crowne of Canterbury." The poet with the same propriety is stationed among "the groomes of . . . [the Archbishop's] stoole." It is "in hope to be preferred" that he undertakes the writing of mar-rimes "for the defence of these honest bishops."[27] That is not an unfounded accusation. Among the "marveilous fitte upholders of Lambehith palace" who, "for one poor penny," are "glad on open stage to play the ignominious fools," are Thomas Nashe and John Lyly and Robert Greene and the facile turncoat, Anthony Munday.

But Martin, in chafing against them, has a more lofty objective in view. Though these are "times lamentable

[26] *Reproofe of Martin Junior*, A2. The content of the seven Marprelate tracts, and of the rejoinders to them, is summarized in Holden (*Anti-Puritan Satire*, pp. 44-52), who appends a bibliography of the controversy.
[27] *Martin Junior's Epilogue*, ? 1589.

to the children of god," he is confident that "the Lord himselfe hath a speciall hand to trye" the persecutors of His children, let them "be who theye are."[28] The thrust at authority is bold enough, and sufficiently clear. "And thinke you not," the poet inquires,

> he will pull down at length
> Aswell the top from tower, as Cocke from steeple?
> And when his head hath gotten some more strength,
>   To play with Prince as now he doth with people:
> Yes, he that now saith, Why should Bishops bee?
> Will next cry out, Why Kings? The Saincts are free.[29]

On either hand, ulteriority governs: for the real point at issue, one must read between the lines. Martin, in his indictment of "the rimers and stageplayers, which my Lords of the cleargy had suborned against me," describes them collectively as "John a Canterbury his hobby-horse."[30] His essential hatred is directed "against both Knights and Lords without regarde."[31] The playwright, in his character of the complaisant retainer, makes "a May game upon the stage" of the Theatre, in which the adversary of the establishment is ridiculed as John the Precise.[32] Elsewhere he is Stupido, or an ass or woodcock or daw.[33] Lyly presents him as an ape to be whipped or a rat to be baned; and Nashe, who is pro-

---

[28] *The Protestatyon of Martin Marprelat,* ? 1589, p. 6.
[29] *Rythmes against Martin Marre-Prelate,* ? 1588, A3.
[30] *Protestatyon,* p. 25.   [31] *Rythmes,* A2v.
[32] *A Merry Knack to Know a Knave,* printed *c.*1594. Munday, who figures in this controversy as a running dog for John Whitgift, the Archbishop of Canterbury, is said to make a May game by Martin in his *Protestatyon.*
[33] *Pilgrimage to Parnassus; Rythmes,* A2.

167

lific on the side of the bishops, as a barking cur that bites behind.[34]

These indignities are more distasteful as the offending poet and playwright are able to escape punishment by taking shelter behind the throne. Joshua, who is the King, "holdes it noe execrable matter to tollerate" plays and players. That is Shakespeare's young colleague, the actor Nathan Field, who wishes to remind a clerical antagonist that "our Caesar our David . . . can vouchsafe amongst his grave exercises some time to tune hymns, and harken unto harmelesse matters of delight." The preacher is "ungodly" (disloyal) who ventures "in a publick pulpitt to say [of the King] that he mainteines those whom God hath damned." Appealing "to the censure of all faithfull subjects," Field argues suavely that the opponent of the stage, in attacking those whom the King has condescended to honor, is necessarily attacking the King himself.[35]

William Prynne, whose scourging of the players is forestalled by the denying of a license, dramatizes this proposition. Prynne is the incarnation of the melodramatic man, who sees in history the contention of *angeli boni* and *angeli mali*. Not unreasonably he is suspected of assigning to the latter pride of place in the history of his own time, in describing as "whorish" the French actresses engaged at Blackfriars by Queen Henrietta

[34] *Pappe with a Hatchet* (prefatory address), 1589; *Pasquill of England*, 1589, A2v. Ribald and violent attacks on the Puritan by Elizabethan poets and playwrights are collected in Holden, *Anti-Puritan Satire*, pp. 52-86, 101-144.

[35] *Feild the Players letter to Mr. Sutton*, 1616, p. 13. The writer is, unexpectedly, the son of that Rev. John Field who had attacked the stage in the Elizabethan period.

Maria (1629). The Queen is not only a patron; she is a player herself, in fact a French player, who dances with the masquers at Whitehall (*The Triumph of Peace*, 1634), as her predecessor in the reign of King James had taken part in Ben Jonson's first courtly entertainment (*The Masque of Blackness*, 1605). The proper title of Prynne's *Histriomastix*, as the Earl of Dorset suggests, is "The Damnation"—not of plays—but "of Prince, Prelacy, Peers and People." The punishment of the foolish man is suited to the magnitude of his folly. By sentence of the Star Chamber, he is taken to the pillory. Both his ears are cut off; the letters S. L. (for Seditious Libeller) are burned in his cheeks. It is an emphatic attesting to the near relation of the theatre and the Crown.

The dissenter takes the relation as given. It is his morose expectation that "Poets and Players shall be Kinges," as they enjoy the King's suffrage: "for the one may lie by authoritie, the other cogge without controle."[36] His anger is high at "the abuses which are committed in suffering of comedies and enterludes." But he has "no hope to see playes forbidden by the magistrats, for commonly they are the first at them."[37] If he writes a treatise "against idle and vaine stage-playes" or "the horrible profanation of the Lords Saboth," it is probable that his work will be "slenderly and slightly regarded of those, whom the Lord hath put in place and authority to punish such greivous sinnes." On the other hand, he

[36] *Fearefull and Lamentable Effects of two dangerous Comets*, p. 11.

[37] Richard Knolles, translating the *Commonwealth* of Jean Bodin, 1606, Bk. VI, pp. 645f.

is sure that "they shalbe . . . called to a strict account one day." The Rule of the Saints is augured, in his advice to the "publique magistrates," that God "will surely take vengeance in time, both on the sinner, and on him that neglecteth to punish the same."[38] That is the eschatologist, who is sustained in the contemplation of ultimate things. Meanwhile, the poet plies his music.

The music of poetry displeases as it enervates. Labor to real purpose is a casualty of "the Commedians stage." The playgoer, who anticipates fruitful instruction, is offered rather "an apprentiship . . . [in] all impudency, loosenesse, whooredome, coozening, deceit and wickednesse."[39] The voice that dins in his ears is "nought but the squeaking out of . . . obscaene and light ligges [lies], stuft with loathsome and unheard-of Ribauldry, suckt from the poisonous dugs of Sinne-sweld Theatres." But what is heard in the theatre is not simply mendacious; it is nugatory: "controversall conferences about richest Beere, neatest Wine, or strongest Tobacco."[40] The preoccupation with trivia is the despair of the eschatologist. His aversion to frivolous deportment ("cakes and ale") is, however, not a function of his Puritanism, in the conventional or vulgar sense, but of his commitment to first and last things.

This commitment supplies the clue to new science. It is manifest in the religious music of the Elizabethans, in the new primacy accorded the Word—and in the plain style of poets like Fulke Greville and Ben Jonson. The distaste for superficies describes the radical Protes-

[38] Rudierde, *Thunderbolt* (abridging the *Theatre of Gods fearefull judgements executed upon notorious sinners*), A2-3.
[39] Knolles' Bodin, p. 645.　　　[40] *This Worlds Folly*, B1v.

tant, like Thomas Cartwright or Beza or Sebastian Franck. He is the type of the winnowing man. What is not so obvious or often remarked is that this same psychology describes the post-Tridentine Catholic. John Rainolds, the Oxford Puritan, writes polemics against the stage. He is an explicable figure and, in formal ways, the antithesis of his older brother William, a Roman Catholic controversialist and professor of divinity and Hebrew at Rheims. But the difference between these two is only formal. William Rainolds, like his brother, is addicted to the Least Common Denominator. See, for instance, his "distillation of the spirits of Turcism out of the books of Calvin." Not less than the Protestant, the latter-day Catholic discerns no profit in the provincial representation. His indifference follows, to "contentions, disputes, and brawles of wordes."[41] In the identification of the surface with trivia, Protestant and Catholic are at one.

The contempt for the surface, and concurrently the insistent concern with the impalpable and generic truth that lies beneath it, is, in this period, not simply an English but a European phenomenon. It is reflected in a waxing hostility to the theatre—in England, from the sixteenth century forward, but also on the Continent: in Protestant Geneva and, impartially, in Catholic France and Spain.[42] To describe this hostility as Puritan is legitimate only as one perceives that much more is at issue than the religion of the sectary—or his aspiration to a fairer place in the sun. Bacon, who is impatient of creeds

[41] A. C. Southern, *Elizabethan Recusant Prose*, p. 257, quoting William Rainolds.
[42] See Barras, *Stage Controversy in France*.

and sects, is a man of the new dispensation, not less than the mystical reformer like Angelus Silesius, or the image breaker like Zwingli: his condemnation of idle shows— the stuffed ox of Prometheus—is of a piece with his endeavor to make reason and the will of God prevail.

Puritanism, in this larger context, is to be taken as a metaphor, emblematizing the hostility of modern man to that indigenous knowledge inhering "in swelling words and painted eloquence of humane wisdome . . . [which is] but a doctrine of the letter." In terms of this metaphor, the Puritan is the devotee of naked truth, who refuses the bone for the marrow, who wants the kernel and is discontent with the shell.[43] The scientist evinces the same discontent. Like the new draconians, in religion, in politics, he distinguishes sharply between the primary and secondary manifestation. Modern science enters Oxford in the train of the New Model Army.[44] The immense prestige it wins in the seventeenth century is, however, not contingent on political change but coeval with it. Neither is a cause but an effect.

The essence of Puritanism, read as a figure emblematic of the modern age, is implied by Archbishop Whitgift in a strikingly suggestive definition:

> The name Puritan is aptly given to these men; not because they be pure, more than were the heretics called Cathari; but because they think themselves to be *mundiores ceteris*, "more pure than others," as Cathari did, and separate themselves from all other churches and congregations, as spotted

[43] Adapted from the Puritan propagandist Henry Holland, editing the sermons of Richard Greenham; quoted in Haller, p. 27.

[44] Christopher Hill, *Puritanism and Revolution*, p. 29.

172

and defiled: because also they suppose the church which they have devised to be without all impurity.[45]

The Cathar or Albigensian who appears in the South of France early in the eleventh century is a disappointed herald, before his time. In the Puritan, his passionate protest against corporeality is resumed. The surface of things, as he construes it, is not alloy but dross. This means, the Incarnation of the Word is a fiction. So with relics and images, and all the physical world, the creation of which is assigned not to God but to Satan. The Cathar is a vegetarian; in theory, a contemner of women. The act of procreation excites his disgust, as it causes the soul to languish in the prison of matter. In his version of the Lord's Prayer, the bread he craves is not daily and palpable but "suprasubstantial bread."

The new Platonist, disusing metaphor and particularization (investigation), is a remote carrier of the early medieval Montanist heresy. He thinks the Truth to be dictated by God to the writer, who is conceived as a passive instrument. St. Jerome and other orthodox medievalists—the adjective is intended as descriptive only in this context—represent God as speaking to the writer, and even of Scripture, not in his ear but in his heart. In other words, one's environment and education, one's temporal and physical milieu do really avail. The artist or, on a lower level, the polemicist is not simply a receiver. The Puritan, as often, is unwilling to assent. In his character of Montanist or new Cathar, the Puritan rejects the intervention of the body, of time and the world. For that reason, he is described—for example,

[45] Quoted in C. and K. George, *Protestant Mind*, pp. 399f.

by the religious and historical writer Sir Richard Baker
(1568-1645)—as "another Montanus . . . come amongst
us."[46] So far, the religious zealot as abstracter or Plato-
nist.

There is, however, another aspect to the comparison
of Puritan and Cathar. Each, as he dissents from the
established religion, is identified with economic protest.
In the medieval lexicon, a weaver is a heretic. In this
respect, at least, what's past is prologue. "I would I were
a weaver," says Falstaff, "I could sing psalms or any-
thing." The equation occurs to Sir Toby, in proposing
a catch to ravish the soul of this pious and industrious
man. In the Renaissance, as in the earlier period, a
weaver is a dissenter. But that is not wholly as the spirit
moves him. It is from the centers of industry and trade
in the eastern counties of England, roughly in the area
from Kent to the Wash and thence to Yorkshire, that
Puritanism recruits the majority of its supporters. Evi-
dently the sectary is not impervious to material con-
siderations. The Waldensians of the twelfth century,
like their Puritan successors four and five centuries later,
disavow the Real Presence in the sacrifice of the Mass—
and recruit their converts primarily from among the
working classes.[47]

The connection persists in sixteenth-century France,
as also in the Netherlands. The artisans in great number
go over to the Huguenot faith; the peasants, as in Eng-
land, remain sympathetic to the faith of their fathers.

[46] Baker, *Theatrum Redivivum*, bet. 1633-38, pp. 125f.; in J. L.
Davis, *Sons of Ben*, p. 41.
[47] Discussion draws on Z. Oldenbourg, *Massacre at Montségur*,
pp. 34-7, 40, 47, 57f., 78f.

Calvinism is apt to flourish where the merchant takes the lead, as in the Dutch-speaking northern provinces of Holland and Zeeland. To the south, in the provinces of Flanders and Brabant where French and Flemish are spoken, the party of privilege maintains its position; Roman Catholicism does also.

The Puritan sings his new song, partly as his eyes are fixed on Heaven. He is also hopeful, like the weaver of Banbury, "To intice Heaven, by singing, to make him lord / Of twenty looms" (William D'Avenant, *The Wits*, 1636). A weaver, then, is a dissenter as he is a covetous man? The suggestion is coarse, and not sufficiently comprehensive. As one interprets historical change as a reflex of the urge to appetitive satisfaction, he will be tempted to diminish or deny altogether the motivating power of the spirit. Brooks Adams, in his great and narrow analyses, is an exemplary case. But the protest against privilege is not exclusively selfish; neither is it confined to the men of reform. Often the party of privilege, and whatever its religious or political cast, is assaulted on altruistic grounds. In the last resort, what is uppermost is the preferring, to the old anarchic world, of a world that is "methodic, regulated, arable; obedient and productive."

The revolutionary ardor that culminates in social and political change is the same ardor that dictates the reformation in dogma, and in ways of reading the world and man's relation to it. The reevaluation of art and its claims is properly to be included in this total congeries, and is in fact a microcosmic representation of the whole. Material self-seeking does not rationalize the whole, but is rather assimilable under the rubric of economics, or utility, writ large. "Political Economy and Social Economy are amusing intellectual games; but Vital Economy is the Philosopher's Stone": Shaw, in his Maxims for Revolutionists.

Vital Economy is the love of Naked Truth. Its opposition is implacable to divagation and waste. In this more inspiriting context, the aristocrat is hateful—and the poet and playwright who run before him—not so much as he is favored but as he is excrescent. The Jacobean businessman, who deprecates the theatre because it is inimical to trade, is an unmysterious figure. Cromwell, on the other hand, is not to be presented as a vulgar opportunist, nor is the revolution he accomplishes explicable merely in terms of the acquisitive instinct. The ardor he communicates is, to a degree, an impersonal ardor. So with the best of the *Mysomousoi* or poet-haters.

Puritanism is attractive to the businessman as he finds the new construction—in morality, theology, esthetics—pat to his disagreeable purpose. In this limited sense, "Weber has . . . completely proved his case."[48] But the case is insufficiently catholic. Puritanism signifies not only Alderman Fowke, who was "not much noted for religion" and was "deeply engaged in Bishops' lands," but Milton and Bunyan and Sir Harry Vane.[49]

The iconoclastic and more fastidious religion which rises with the Renaissance and which is not, on my reading, exclusively Protestant, does not prepare the way for a new social order, but is another exemplification of

[48] Ernst Troeltsch (*Protestantism and Progress*, pp. 132-38), whose opinion varies elsewhere.
[49] Hill, *Puritanism*, p. 29.

176

the same spirit which brings this order to birth. Calvinism, in the beginning, attracts a large following from the older aristocracy and is, in the beginning, incurious of social questions. The identification with a particular class is neither apparent nor mandatory.[50] The great economist who wills an end to the dark epoch before his own and the inutile diversions by which it is recognized is not the grasping tradesman, whom we have always with us, but the modern regisseur, not Melton or Cranfield but Bacon and Sprat and Descartes. The impulse to personal advancement is a larcenous impulse, and hence of no particular interest. The impulse to economy and rigorous form is, however, artistic: impersonal, and definitive of the new or renascent age.

It is tenable but provincial to speak of the making of the modern world in terms of the contest of classes. A part is apprehended as doing duty for the whole. In this cursory fashion, the historian presents the metamorphosis of the medieval Parliament, which he sees as converted to "an instrument of class power directed against king, court, and the barons."[51] The observation does not take one very far. For this new and powerful instrument is often exercised in ways that owe allegiance, not to class, but to a higher imperative. It is true that, on the eve of Civil War, the greatest number of families in the "political nation" were rising families, with less than three generations of eminence behind them. Without question they had cause to seek to cancel "such obsolete laws and customs as hampered their rise, and to dislike

[50] The observation of Troeltsch, *Social Teaching of the Christian Churches*, ii, 646.

[51] C. and K. George, *Protestant Mind*, pp. 14f.

the wealth and the ways of their betters."[52] But these nouveaux riches, in the teeth of simple expectation, side indifferently with Parliament or Crown. The contending parties in 1640 do not divide in every case along the lines of social class and economic affiliation. Sometimes the merchant cleaves to the King, while the knight and the baronet forsake him.[53] A modern interpreter of the revolutionary period sees in this fact no special significance: Lords and Commons are divided because the ruling class is divided.[54] But how does one explain the choosing up of sides? "What is it that makes one great-grandson of a Tudor copyholder or a Tudor judge a progressive bourgeois, and another a feudal aristocrat?"[55] Crudely selfish motivation does not account for the emergence of the modern world, but is only one among feodary causes. On a comprehensive view, perhaps it is the least interesting.

Modern or progressive man is elusive in his politics, and not to be described—or not infallibly—as Royalist or Roundhead. The decisive thrust which moves him, and distinguishes present from past, is the zeal for perspicuous truth. This is the real and perdurable tie which binds together the new men—whatever the social and political views which would appear to separate one from another—and announces their separation from the old or myopic age.

The same proposition holds of religion. The more fiery variant of Puritanism reflects the claims of the "un-

[52] D. Brunton and D. H. Pennington, *Members of the Long Parliament*, p. 181.
[53] Brunton and Pennington, p. 177.
[54] Hill, p. 20.   [55] Brunton and Pennington, p. 178.

178

enfranchised" and is fueled by an angry sense of "social inequity." And yet in religion, in politics also, there are "those upon the Royalist side who in matters of doctrine were ancestors of the Whigs."[56] No doubt there exists, in the English Protestant conception of the saint, "an element of social subversion." But the saint himself, in his social teachings, is not radical or egalitarian. Mostly, he enacts the role of embittered conservative. "*Renovatores modo sumus, non Novatores,*" says Bishop Lancelot Andrewes.[57]

Reaction stamps and identifies the writing of the religious reformer. So much is incontestable: the religious literature of the period—vast in its extent and monomaniacally consistent in its point of view—is my warrant here. The nostalgic or reactionary man is, nonetheless, the agent of revolutionary change: not because he is covetous of personal aggrandizement but because he wills an end to the insufficient life for all his fellows and compels their allegiance to the City of God on earth. Like Plato, in whom this ruthlessly humanitarian temperament is supremely fulfilled, he is inspired by a hatred of superficies and, sequentially, a desire to delve below the surface of things. Below the surface is the truth that avails.

The connoisseur of first and last things, in his character of militant salvationist, seeks to banish the poet and playwright because, in their commitment to the phe-

[56] Mathew, *Social Structure in Caroline England*, pp. 10, 88f.

[57] C. and K. George, pp. 92-4, 104. Andrewes is quoted, p. 382. For the political and social conservatism of English Protestant divines, and the essential continuity with the Puritan point of view, see pp. 174-210, 216-21, 372.

nomenal or merely figurative representation, they are involved with no more than a cantle of the truth. This heretical understanding of poetry, as enunciated first of all by Plato and made canonical in the Renaissance, is essentially the modern understanding. That is one consequence of the war against poetry. "These," says the modern critic very laconically—he is approving what he takes to be the perspicuous language of *Hamlet*—"are no poetic similes, but keen observations of reality."[58] Shakespeare perhaps is *sui generis*. Other poets displease, says a famous historian, as "their happiest sentiments are frequently involved in . . . a cloud of metaphor." To body forth is to falsify. "How far superior is one touch of nature," defined as *nuda veritas* or the thing itself, "to all this farrago of metaphor and mythology!"[59]

The poet and playwright, as they pursue the metaphorical way, abandon the real world for the *selva oscura* of fable and romance: the criticism of Tyndale. They do not "move to Vertue . . . [but] stirre up the mind to shady idlenesse." The putative eloquence which the coarser past attributes to them is "vaine eloquence." The eschatologist or truth-telling man, as his sensibilities are finer, is not much inclined to listen. In his assessment of "Enterludes and Playes," he requires us "to thrust them out as things indifferent."[60]

This requirement does not govern until the Renaissance. The era which the Renaissance stigmatizes as the

[58] W. H. Clemen, *Development of Shakespeare's Imagery*, pp. 106-18.
[59] Prescott, *Ferdinand and Isabella*, I, 22.
[60] Henry Crosse in *Vertues Common-wealth*, O1-P2.

Dark Ages has apparently no studied end in view, unless it is the salvation of souls. Lassitude is of its essence. It does not suppose that *progress* is definable, except as a royal progress. As that is so, it is *antiquated, out-of-date,* or *primeval*—words which come to birth in the seventeenth century. Or it is, in the complacent phrase of a literary historian, "*cette longue nuit de sommeil et de rêve.*"[61] There is propriety in its reception of "vaine, idle, wanton Pamphlets and lascivious love-bookes." These are bred by the epitome of medieval man, "the lazy Monkes, & fat-headed Friers, in whom was nothing but sloathe & idlenes."[62]

But now, in the energetic age that supervenes, men "must render an account for every idle word."[63] This accounting is mandatory, from the late sixteenth century forward. Now "the Active is to bee preferred before the Contemplative."[64] The homiletic writer who asserts its priority is very modern in supposing that as "vertue is the life of action," so "action [is] the life of man."[65] The active life is intentional. It is the business of the Renaissance to accomplish that progress which man in the Middle Ages denies. Virtue is discovered in the building of the kingdom, not over yonder but in the here and now. With this discovery, the modern age begins.

[61] Symmes, *Les Débuts*, Ch. i.   [62] Crosse, N4.
[63] R. Junius, *Compleat Armour Against Evil Society*, p. 824.
[64] *English Gentleman*, p. 308.   [65] *English Gentlewoman*, p. 28.

Works Consulted

I have not listed well-known authors who are quoted in the text—like Bacon, Gibbon, St. Augustine, Ben Jonson—unless reference is to page or signature number in a particular edition. STC numbers (for books printed between 1475 and 1640) and Wing numbers (between 1641 and 1700) are appended, where available.

Adams, Robert P. "Bold Bawdry and Open Manslaughter: The English New Humanist Attack on Medieval Romance," *Huntington Library Quarterly*, XXIII, 1959-1960, 33-48.

Adams, Thomas. *The Gallants Burden, A Sermon preached at Paules Crosse, The Twentie nine of March . . . 1612*, London, 1612. STC 117.

———. *The Workes of*, London, 1629. STC 104.

Agrippa, Henry Cornelius. *The Vanitie and Uncertaintie of Arts and Sciences*, trans. Ja. [mes] San [ford], London, 1569. STC 204.

Ames, William. *Conscience with the Power and Cases Thereof*, trans. from Latin, London, 1639, ? 1643. STC 552.

Ante-Nicene, Nicene, and Post-Nicene Fathers of The Christian Church, ed. Alexander Roberts, James Donaldson, A. C. Coxe, Philip Schaff, *et al.*, 38 vols., Grand Rapids, Mich., 1956.

Anthony, Sister Rose. *The Jeremy Collier Stage Controversy 1698-1726* (1937), New York, 1966.

Anton, Robert. *Vices Anotimie, Scourged and Corrected, in New Satirs*, London, 1617. STC 687.

Atkins, J.W.H. *English Literary Criticism: The Medieval Phase*, New York and Cambridge, 1943.

Averell, William. *A Dyall for Dainty Darlings*, London, 1584. STC 978.

Babington, Gervase. *A Very Fruitfull Exposition of the Commandments by way of Questions and Answers*, London, 1583. STC 1095.

Bainton, Roland H. *The Reformation of the Sixteenth Century*, Boston, 1952.

Baker, Herschel. *The Wars of Truth*, Cambridge, Mass., 1952.

Baldwin, Frances Elizabeth. *Sumptuary Legislation and Personal Regulation in England*, Baltimore, 1926.

Barfield, Owen. *History in English Words (1953)*, Grand Rapids, Mich., 1967.

Barish, Jonas A. "Exhibitionism and the Anti-Theatrical Prejudice," *English Literary History*, XXXVI, No. 1 (1969), 1-29.

———. "The Antitheatrical Prejudice," *Critical Quarterly*, VIII (1966), 329-48.

Barras, Moses. *The Stage Controversy in France from Corneille to Rousseau*, New York, 1933.

Bayly, Lewis. *The Practise of pietie*, London, 1613. STC 1602.

Beard, Charles A., and Mary R. *The Rise of American Civilization (1927)*, 2 vols., New York, 1947.

Bedford Arthur. *The Evil and Danger of Stage-Plays: Shewing their Natural Tendency to Destroy Religion, and Introduce a General Corruption of Manners; In almost Two Thousand Instances*, London, 1706.

———. *A Serious Remonstrance in Behalf of the Christian Religion, Against the Horrid Blasphemies and Impieties which are still used in the English Play-Houses*, London, 1719.

Bentley, Gerald Eades. *Shakespeare and His Theatre*, Lincoln, Neb., 1964.

Bevington, David. *Tudor Drama and Politics: A Critical Approach to Topical Meaning*, Cambridge, Mass., 1968.

Boas, Frederick S. *University Drama in the Tudor Age*, Oxford, 1914.

Boccaccio on Poetry, trans. Charles G. Osgood (1930), Indianapolis and New York, 1956.

Bodin, Jean. *The Six Bookes of a Common-weale*, trans. Richard Knolles, London, 1606. STC 3193.

Bolton, Robert. *A Discourse About the State of True Happinesse*, London, 1612. STC 3229.

————. *Some Generall Directions for a Comfortable Walking with God*, London, 1625. STC 3250.

Bowen, Catherine Drinker. *The Lion and the Throne. The Life and Times of Sir Edward Coke (1552-1634)*, Boston, 1956.

Bownd, Nicholas. *The Doctrine of the Sabbath pluinely layde forth*, London, 1595. STC 3436.

Brasbridge, Thomas. *The poore mans jewel, that is to say a treatise of the pestilence*, London, 1578. STC 3549.

Brathwait, Richard. *The English Gentleman*, 2nd ed., London, 1633. STC 3564.

————. *The English Gentleman and the English Gentlewoman*, London, 1641. Wing 4262.

————. *The English Gentlewoman*, London, 1631. STC 3565.

Brinsley, John The Elder. *The True Watch and Rule of Life*, London, 1622 (*The Third Part of the True-Watch or The Call of the Lord*, London, 1623). STC 3787.

Brooke, Tucker. "The Stage and Public Morality," in A. C. Baugh, ed., *A Literary History of England*, New York and London, 1948, pp. 441-45.

Brown, Norman O. *Life Against Death*, New York, 1959.

Brunton, D., and D. H. Pennington. *Members of the Long Parliament*, introduction by R. H. Tawney, London, 1954.

Bryskett, Lodowick. *A Discourse of Civill Life*, London, 1606. STC 3958.

Bryson, Frederick R. *The Point of Honor in Sixteenth-Century Italy: An Aspect of the Life of the Gentleman*, Chicago, 1933.

Buchan, John. *Oliver Cromwell* (1934), London, 1957.

Burton, Henry. *For God, and the King* (two sermons preached 5 Nov. last), London, 1636. STC 4141.

Caesarius of Heisterbach. *The Dialogue of Miracles*, Vol. I, trans. H. Scott and C. Bland, London, 1929.

Calendar of State Papers, Domestic Series Edward VI to James I. 1547-1625, 12 vols., ed. Robert Lemon and M.A.E. Green, London, 1856-1872; *Charles I. 1627-1629*, 2 vols., ed. John Bruce, London, 1858-1859.

Chamberlain, John. *The Letters of*, 2 vols., ed. Norman E. McClure, Phila., 1939.

Chambers, E. K., ed. "Dramatic Records of the City of London: The Repertories, Journals, and Letter Books," *Malone Society Collections*, II, Pt. III, Oxford, 1931, 285-320.

――――. *The Elizabethan Stage*, 4 vols. (1923), Oxford, 1961.

――――. *English Literature at the Close of the Middle Ages*, Oxford, 1945.

――――. *The Mediaeval Stage*, 2 vols., Oxford, 1903.

――――. and W. W. Greg, eds. "Dramatic Records from the Lansdowne Manuscripts," *Malone Society Collections*, I, Pt. II, Oxford, 1908, 143-215.

Chettle, Henry. *Kind-Harts Dreame*, London [1592]. STC 5123.

Chute, Marchette. *Ben Jonson of Westminster*, New York, 1953.

Clemen, W. H. *The Development of Shakespeare's Imagery*, Cambridge, Mass., 1951.

Clement, Francis. *The Petie Schole with an English Orthographie*, London, 1587. STC 5400.

Clements, Robert J. "Condemnation of the Poetic Profession in Renaissance Emblem Literature," *Studies in Philology*, XLIII, 1946, 213-32.

Collier, Jeremy. *A Defence of the Short View of the Profaneness and Immorality of the English Stage,* London, 1699. Wing 5248.

————. *A Short View of the Immorality, and Profaneness of the English Stage,* London, 1698. Wing 5263.

Collinson, Patrick. *The Elizabethan Puritan Movement,* Berkeley and Los Angeles, 1967.

Court and Times of Charles the First, The, ed. R. F. Williams, 2 vols., London, 1848.

Covenant between God and Man, The, see F., I.

Craig, Hardin. *English Religious Drama of the Middle Ages,* Oxford, 1955.

Cram, Ralph Adams. *Walled Towns,* Boston, 1919.

Crashaw, William. *The Parable of Poyson. In Five Sermons,* London, 1618. STC 6024.

————. *A Sermon Preached in London before the . . . Captain Generall of Virginea,* London, 1610. STC 6029.

————. *The Sermon Preached at the Crosse, Feb. xiiij. 1607,* London, 1608. STC 6027.

Crosse, Henry. *Vertuos Common-wealth: or The High-way to Honour,* London, 1603. STC 6070.

Cullen, Charles. "Puritanism and the Stage," *Proceedings of the Royal Philosophical Society of Glasgow,* XLIII, 1911-1912, 153-81.

Davis, Joe Lee. *The Sons of Ben: Jonsonian Comedy in Caroline England,* Detroit, Mich., 1967.

Dering, Edward. *A bryefe and necessarie Catechisme or Instruction,* London, 1572-1577. STC 6679.

Donald, M. B. *Elizabethan Monopolies,* Edinburgh and London, 1961.

Ehrenberg, Richard. *Capital & Finance in the Age of the Renaissance: A Study of the Fuggers and Their Connections* (*Das Zeitalter der Fugger*), trans. H. M. Lucas (1928), New York, 1963.

187

Eiseley, Loren. *Francis Bacon and the Modern Dilemma*. Lincoln, Neb., 1962.

F., I. *The Covenant between God and Man*, London, 1616. STC 10639.

F., T. [Thomas Ford]. *Newes from the North. Otherwise called the Conference between Simon Certain and Pierce Plowman*, London, 1585. STC 24062ᵃ.

Farrar, Frederic W. *History of Interpretation* (1886), Grand Rapids, Mich., 1961.

Fenner, Dudley. *A Short and profitable Treatise, of lawfull and unlawfull Recreations*, Middleburgh, 1587. STC 10776.

Field [or Feilde], John. *A Godly Exhortation by occasion of the late judgement of God*, London, 1583. STC 10845.

Field, Nathan. *The Remonstrance . . . Addressed to a Preacher in Southwark, Who Had Been Arraigning Against the Players at the Globe Theatre in . . . 1616*, London, 1865 (MS entitled: *Feild the players letters to Mr. Sutton, preacher at St. Mary Overs., 1616*).

Fisher, F. J. "The Development of London as a Centre of Conspicuous Consumption in the Sixteenth and Seventeenth Centuries," *Transactions of the Royal Historical Society*, 4th ser., xxx, London, 1948, 37-50.

Friedrich, Carl J. *The Age of the Baroque 1610-1660*, New York, 1952.

Fromm, Erich. *Escape from Freedom*, New York and Toronto, 1941.

Fuller, Thomas. *The Holy State*, Cambridge, 1642. Wing 2443.

G., I. *A Refutation of the Apology for Actors* (1615); with Heywood's *Apology* (1612), ed. Richard H. Perkinson, New York, 1941.

George, Charles H. and Katherine. *The Protestant Mind of the English Reformation 1570-1640*, Princeton, 1961.

Gerth, H. H., and C. Wright Mills. *From Max Weber*, New York, 1958.

Gildersleeve, Virginia C. *Government Regulation of the Eliza-bethan Drama*, New York, 1908.

Googe, Barnabe, trans. Marcellus Palingenius: *the Zodyake of lyfe*, London, 1560.

Gosson, Stephen. *The Ephemerides of Phialo. . . . And a short Apologie of the Schoole of Abuse, against Poets, Pipers, Players & their Excusers*, London, 1579. STC 12093.

————. *Playes Confuted in five Actions, Proving that they are not to be suffred in a Christian common weale, by the waye both the Cavils of Thomas Lodge, and the Play of Playes, written in their defence, and other objections of Players frendes, are truely set downe and directlye aunswered*, London [? 1590]. STC 12095.

————. *The Schoole of Abuse*, London, 1579. STC 12097.

Graves, Thornton S. "Notes on Puritanism and the Stage," *Studies in Philology*, XVIII, 2, April 1921, 141-69.

————. "The Political Use of the Stage During the Reign of James I," *Anglia*, XXXVIII (1914), 137-56.

H., J. *This Worlds Folly*, London, 1615. STC 12570.

Halevy, Elie. *The Growth of Philosophic Radicalism* (1901-1904), Boston, 1955.

Hall, John. *The Court of Virtue*, London, 1565 (ed. R. A. Fraser, London, 1961). STC 12632.

Haller, William. *The Rise of Puritanism* (1938), New York, 1957.

Harbage, Alfred. *Shakespeare's Audience*, New York, 1941.

Harrison, William. *An Historical Description of the Islande of Britayne*, in Holinshed's *Chronicles*, Vol. 1, London, 1577. STC 13568.

Hazlitt, William Carew, ed. *The English Drama and Stage under the Tudor and Stuart Princes 1543-1664 Illustrated by a Series of Documents, Treatises and Poems* (1869), New York, n.d. (Burt Franklin Research and Source Works Series #48.)

Herbert, Sir Henry, The Dramatic Records of, ed. J. Q. Adams, New Haven, 1917.

Hill, Christopher. *Puritanism and Revolution* (1958), New York, 1964.

Hill, Robert. *The Pathway to Prayer and Pietie*, London, 1613. STC 13473.

Hilliard, Nicholas. *A Treatise Concerning the Arte of Limning* (1624), Oxford, 1912.

Holden, William P. *Anti-Puritan Satire 1572-1642*, New Haven, 1954.

Howell, Roger. *Sir Philip Sidney The Shepherd Knight*, London, 1968.

Hubler, Edward. *The Sense of Shakespeare's Sonnets*, Princeton, 1952.

Huizinga, Johan. *The Waning of the Middle Ages* (1924), New York, 1954.

Hunter, G. K. *John Lyly The Humanist as Courtier*, London, 1962.

Johnson, S. F. pp. 210-12 in O. J. Campbell, *Reader's Encyclopedia of Shakespeare*, New York, 1966.

Jordan, W. K. *Philanthropy in England 1480-1660*, New York, 1959.

Junius, R. [?Richard Younge]. *Compleat Armour Against Evill Society*, London, 1638. STC 26111.

Kelso, Ruth. *The Doctrine of the English Gentleman in the Sixteenth Century*, University of Illinois Studies in Language and Literature, XIV (1929), 1-288.

Ker, W. P. *The Dark Ages* (1904), New York, 1958.

Keynes, J. M. *A Treatise on Money*, 2 vols., New York, 1930.

Knappen, M. M. *Tudor Puritanism A Chapter in the History of Idealism* (1938), Gloucester, Mass., 1963.

Knights, L. C. *Drama and Society in the Age of Jonson*, London, 1937.

————. "Education and the Drama in the Age of Shakespeare," *Criterion*, XI (1931-1932), 599-625.

Knox, Bernard M. W. *Oedipus at Thebes*, New Haven, 1957.

Lake, Osmund. *A Probe Theologicall*, London, 1612. STC 15136.

Latham, Ronald E. *Revised Medieval Latin Word-List*, London, 1965.

Law, William. *The Absolute Unlawfulness of the Stage-Entertainment*, London, 1726.

Lenton, Francis. *The Young Gallants Whirligigg*, London, 1629. STC 15467.

Lewis, Wyndham. *The Lion and the Fox*, New York and London, n.d.

Lodge, Thomas. *A Reply to Stephen Gosson's Schoole of Abuse, in Defense of Poetry, Musick, and Stage Plays*, London, 1579-1580, no t.p., no imprint. STC 16663. Reprinted London, 1853 (with Lodge's *Alarum against Usurers*, 1584).

——. *Wits Miserie, and the Worlds Madnesse*, London, 1596. STC 16677.

Lupton, Thomas. *Sivqila* [i.e., Aliquis], *Too good, to be true*, London, 1580. STC 16951.

Luther, Martin. *Works*, ed. Jaroslav Pelikan and Helmut T. Lehmann, 31 vols., St. Louis, Mo., 1955——.

Martin Marprelate. "The Description of a Puritan," appended to *A Dialogue Wherein Is Plainly Layd Opon The Tyrannicall Dealing of Lord Bishops . . . by . . . Dr. Martin Marprelate*, n.p., 1643. (*The Dialogue*, without "Description," was apparently first printed in 1589.) STC 17460.

——. *The just censure and reproofe of Martin Jnr . . . by his reverend and elder brother*, n.p., n.d. [? Wolston, ? 1589]. STC 17458.

——. *The Marprelate Tracts, 1588, 1589*, ed. William Pierce, London, 1911.

——. *Martin Junior's Epilogue*, n.p., n.d. [? Wolston, ? 1589]. STC 17457.

——. *The Protestatyon of Martin Marprelat*, n.p., n.d. [? Wolston, ? 1589]. STC 17459.

Martin Marprelate. *Rythmes against Martin Marre-Prelate*, n.p., n.d. [?1588]. STC 17465.

Mathew, David. *The Social Structure in Caroline England*, Oxford, 1948.

Melton, John. *A Sixe-Folde Politician*, London, 1609. STC 17805.

Mesnard, Pierre. "The Pedagogy of Johann Sturm (1507-1589) and Its Evangelical Inspiration," *Studies in the Renaissance*, XIII (1966), 200-19.

Miller, Edwin Haviland. *The Professional Writer in Elizabethan England: A Study of Nondramatic Literature*, Cambridge, Mass., 1959.

More, Sir Thomas. *The Complete Works*, Vol. II, *The history of king Richard III*, ed. Richard S. Sylvester, New Haven, 1963.

Munday, Anthony [probable author]. *A Second and third blast of retrait from plaies and Theatres*, London, 1580.

———. *See* C. T. Wright.

Myers, Aaron M. *Representation and Misrepresentation of the Puritan in Elizabethan Drama*, Phila., 1931.

Nagler, A. M., *Shakespeare's Stage*, New Haven, 1958.

Nashe, Thomas. *Pierce Penilesse*, London, 1592. STC 18371.

Neal, Daniel. *The History of the Puritans*, 2 vols., New York, 1848.

Nelson, Benjamin N. *The Idea of Usury*, Princeton, 1949.

Nixon, Anthony. *The Black-yeare*, London, 1606. STC 18582.

Norden, John. *A progresse of pietie*, London, 1596. STC 18633.

Northbrooke, John. *A Treatise wherein Dicing, Dauncing, Vaine plaies or Enterludes with other idle pastimes . . . are reprooved*, London, 1579. STC 18671.

Oldenbourg, Zoe. *Massacre at Montségur: A History of the Albigensian Crusade*, London, 1961.

Origo, Iris. *The Merchant of Prato, Francesco di Marco Datini 1335-1410*, New York, 1957.

Peacham, Henry the Younger. *The Compleat Gentleman* (1622), ed. G. S. Gordon, Oxford, 1906.

Perkins, William. *A Case of Conscience*, n.p., 1595. STC 19667.

Pirenne, Henri. *A History of Europe*, 2 vols., Garden City, New York, 1956.

Platter, Thomas. *Travels in England, 1599*, trans. Clare Williams, London, 1937.

Prescott, William H. *History of Ferdinand and Isabella*, 3 vols., Boston, 1856.

Primaudaye, Peter de la. *The French Academy*, trans. T. B., London, 1586, 1594.

Prynne, William. *Histrio-Mastix*, London, 1633. STC 20464.

Quarles, Francis. *Divine fancies; digested into epigrammes, meditations, and observations*, London, 1632. STC 20529.

Rainolds, John. *Sex Theses de Sacra Scriptura et Ecclesia*, London, 1580. STC 20624.

————. *The Summe of the Conference between John Rainolds and John Hart. . . . Whereto is annexed a Treatise intitled, Six Conclusions Touching the Holie Scripture and the Church*, London, 1584. STC 20626.

————. *Th'Overthrow of Stage-Playes*, Middleburg, 1599. STC 20616.

Ramsey, Peter. *Tudor Economic Problems*, London, 1963.

Rankins, William. *The mirrour of monsters: wherein is described the vices caused by sight of playes*, London, 1587. STC 20699.

Representation of the Impiety and Immorality of the English Stage, A, Anon., London, 1704.

Ridpath, George. *The Stage Condemned*, n.p., 1698. Wing 1468.

Ringler, William. "The First Phase of the Elizabethan Attack on the Stage, 1558-1579," *Huntington Library Quarterly*, V (1941-1942), 391-418.

————. *Stephen Gosson: A Biographical and Critical Study*, Princeton, 1942.

R. R. [Richard Rogers]. *The Practice of Christianitie*, London, 1618, 1623. STC 21221.

Romei, Annibale. *The Courtiers Academie*, trans. I. K., n.p., n.d. [?London, 1598]. STC 21311.

Rosenberg, Eleanor. *Leicester Patron of Letters*, New York, 1955.

Rosenfeld, Sybil M. *Strolling Players Drama in the Provinces 1660-1765*, Cambridge, 1939.

Rossiter, A. P. *English Drama from Early Times to the Elizabethans*, London, 1950.

Rowe, John. *Tragi-Comaedia, Being a Brief Relation of the Strange, and Wonderfull hand of God discovered at Witney*, Oxford, 1653. Wing 2067.

Rudierde, Edmund. *The Thunderbolt of Gods Wrath against Hard-Hearted and stiffe-necked sinners*, London, 1618. STC 21437.

Schaar, Claes. *On the Motif of Death in Sixteenth-Century Sonnet Poetry*, Scripta Minora, Lund, 1959-1960.

Semper, I. J. "The Jacobean Theater through the Eyes of Catholic Clerics," *Shakespeare Quarterly* III (1952), 45-51.

Shaw, William A. *The Knights of England*, 2 vols., London, 1906.

Sheavyn, Phoebe. *The Literary Profession in the Elizabethan Age* (1909), revised by J. W. Saunders, Manchester and New York, 1967.

Sidney, Sir Philip. *The Prose Works*, ed. Albert Feuillerat, 4 vols. (1912), Cambridge, 1962.

Siebert, Frederick S. *Freedom of the Press in England 1476-1776*, Urbana, Ill., 1952.

Simpson, Alan. *Puritanism in Old and New England*, Chicago, 1955.

———. *The Wealth of the Gentry, 1540-1660*, Cambridge and Chicago, 1961.

Smel-Knave, Simon. *Fearefull and Lamentable Effects of two dangerous Comets*, London, ? 1590. STC 22645.

Smith, G. Gregory, ed. *Elizabethan Critical Essays*, 2 vols. (1904), Oxford, 1950.

Southern, A. C. *Elizabethan Recusant Prose 1559-1582*, London and Glasgow, 1950.

Sprat, Thomas. *History of the Royal Society*, 1667, ed. Jackson I. Cope and Harold Whitmore Jones, St. Louis, Mo., 1958.

Stevens, John. *Music & Poetry in the Early Tudor Court*, Lincoln, Neb., 1963.

Stockwood, John. *A sermon preached at Paules Crosse on Barthelmew day*, London, 1578. STC 23284.

Stone, Lawrence. "The Anatomy of the Elizabethan Aristocracy," *Economic History Review*, XVIII, nos. 1 and 2 (1948), 1-53.

———. *The Crisis of the Aristocracy*, Oxford, 1965.

———. "A Restatement," *Economic History Review*, 2nd ser., IV (1952), 302-21.

———. ed. *Social Change and Revolution in England 1540-1640*, London, 1965.

Stow, John. *Survey of London*, London, 1618. STC 23344.

Stubbes, Philip. *The Anatomie of Abuses*, London, 1583. STC 23376.

Summe of Sacred Divinitie, The (pub. by John Downhame), London, c. 1630.

Symmes, H. S. *Les Débuts de la Critique Dramatique en Angleterre*, Paris, 1903.

Tarleton, Dick, *see* Chettle.

Tawney, Richard Henry. *The Agrarian Problem in the Sixteenth Century*, London, 1912.

———. *Business and Politics under James I: Lionel Cranfield As Merchant and Minister*, Cambridge, 1958.

———. *Religion and the Rise of Capitalism* (1926), London, 1948.

Tawney, Richard Henry. "The Rise of the Gentry, 1558-1640," *Economic History Review*, XI (1941), 1-38.

―――. "The Rise of the Gentry: A Postscript," *Economic History Review*, 2nd ser., VII, no. 1 (1954), 91-97.

Thompson, Elbert N. S. *The Controversy between the Puritans and the Stage*, New York, 1903.

Treatise of Daunses, A, Wherein it is showed, that they are as it were accessories and dependants . . . to whoredom: where also by the way is touched and proved, that Playes are joyned and knit together in a ranck or rowe with them, Anon., ? London, 1581.

Trevor-Roper, H. R. "The Elizabethan Aristocracy: An Anatomy Anatomized," *Economic History Review*, 2nd ser., III (1951), 279-98.

Troeltsch, Ernst. *Protestantism and Progress; a historical study of the relation of Protestantism to the modern world*, trans. W. Montgomery, New York, 1912.

―――. *The Social Teaching of the Christian Churches* (1911), trans. Olive Wyon (1931), 2 vols., New York, 1960.

Twyne, Thomas, trans. *Phisicke against Fortune, as well prosperous as adverse*, n.p., 1579.

Tyndale, William. *Obedyence of a Chrysten man*, n.p., n.d. [? Marburg, ? 1536]. STC 24447.

Upton, Anthony F. *Sir Arthur Ingram: A Study of the Origins of an English Landed Family*, Oxford, 1961.

Valency, Maurice. *In Praise of Love. An Introduction to the Love-Poetry of the Renaissance*, New York, 1958.

Vaughan, William. *The Golden Grove*, London, 1608. STC 24611.

―――. *The Spirit of Detraction*, London, 1611. STC 24622.

W., T. [Thomas White?]. "A Sermon Preached at Paules Crosse on Sunday the thirde of November 1577. in the time of the Plague," London, 1578. STC 24918.

Waddell, Helen, trans. *The Desert Fathers* (1936), Ann Arbor, Mich., 1957.

Walsal, John. *A Sermon Preached at Pauls Crosse,* 5 Oct. 1578, London, 1578. STC 24995.

Watson, Curtis Brown. *Shakespeare and the Renaissance Concept of Honor,* Princeton, 1960.

Weber, Max, *see* Gerth and Mills.

―――――. *The Protestant Ethic and the Spirit of Capitalism,* London, 1930.

Webster, John. *Academiarum Examen,* London, 1653 [t.p. reads 1654]. Wing 1209.

Wedgewood, C. V. *Poetry and Politics Under the Stuarts* (1960), Ann Arbor, Mich., 1964.

Wells, John Edwin. *A Manual of the Writings in Middle English, 1050-1400,* New Haven, 1916.

Whetstone, George. *A Touchstone for the Time* (in *A mirour for magestrates of cyties*), London, 1584. STC 25341.

Whitney, Geoffrey. *A Choice of Emblemes,* Leyden, 1586. STC 25438.

Wickham, Glynne. *Early English Stages:* Vol. I, *1300-1576;* Vol. II, Pt. I, *1578-1660,* London, 1963.

Williams, Franklin B., Jr. *Index of Dedications and Commendatory Verses in English Books before 1641,* London, The Bibliographical Society, 1962.

Wilson, J. Dover. "The Puritan Attack Upon the Stage," *Cambridge History of English Literature* (1910), Vol. VI, Pt. 2, New York and Cambridge, 1932, 421-61.

Wilson, Thomas. *A Discourse upon Usury,* 1572, with an historical introduction by R. H. Tawney, London, 1925.

Winspear, Alban D. *The Genesis of Plato's Thought,* New York, 1940.

Wither, George. *Abuses Stript, and Whipt,* London, 1613. STC 25891.

197

Witherspoon, John. *A Serious Enquiry into the Nature & Effects of the Stage*, Glasgow, 1762.

Wright, Celeste Turner. *Anthony Munday An Elizabethan Man of Letters*, University of California Publications in English, II, no. 1, Berkeley, 1928, 1-234.

Wright, Louis B. *Middle Class Culture in Elizabethan England*, London, 1935.

Young, Karl. *The Drama of the Medieval Church* (1933), 2 vols., Oxford, 1962.

————. "William Gager's Defence of the Academic Stage," *Transactions of the Wisconsin Academy of Sciences, Arts, and Letters*, XVIII, Pt. II (1916), 593-638.

Index

Publications first appearing in the twentieth century, and footnoted in the text, are not entered in this Index. Authors of such publications are, however, entered; as are the titles and authors of all older books.

199